A common assumption among church l
say on organising and leading our chur
these pastor theologians demonstrate
this book provides exactly what evange ... .uanity needs, but generally
doesn't know it: a biblical vision for robust and healthy churches. Not only that,
the authors' pastoral wisdom will encourage and challenge readers on every
page. Buy two copies – one for yourself and another for a fellow church leader.
I'm confident you'll be glad you did. So will your church.

Jonathan Leeman, Editorial Director, 9Marks

Historically, Baptists took the doctrine of the church very seriously. However,
ecclesiology has been the Cinderella of evangelicalism for the past fifty years
or more. It is therefore great to see a generation of Baptist pastors once more
concerned to argue for and spell out the biblical teaching on the life and
order of the local church. This short and accessible book makes an invaluable
contribution to the rediscovery of a biblically vibrant local church life. Read it,
teach it, study it and put into practice the principles that it expounds.

Robert Strivens, Pastor of Bradford on Avon Baptist Church

The renewal of interest in Baptist ecclesiology in recent years has been the
cause of much rejoicing among members of Grace Baptist churches in the UK.
Articles have been written. Books have been published. Conferences have been
organised. One thing, however, is worth noting. A lot of the available material
has had a distinctly American accent. I realise truth is truth regardless of
accent, but it is helpful to hear those truths articulated by those who have not
only similar biblical convictions but who share the same cultural context as
well.

Written at an accessible level in a warm and engaging manner, these
writers – all based in the UK – clearly communicate the gospel order they
desire to see recovered by the churches. This work is not just for leaders but for
church members as well. You may not agree with every position taken. But you
will be hard-pressed to fault the disposition of the writers. They have sought to
write wisely and winsomely for the glory of God and the good of the churches.

**Barry King, Pastor of Dunstable Baptist Church and General Secretary of Grace
Baptist Partnership**

It is great to have a book that so positively endorses life in a local church. The authors work from Scripture to paint a picture of what a community of Christians should and can look like. The inner reality of genuine Christian experience is matched with the proper ordering and structuring of that life so that a thriving church is the result. It has long been my conviction that we need to marry, in effect, an 'Acts 2' description of church life with an 'Acts 6' development of good structure. This book takes that idea and works it out much more widely, and with reference to many issues. Anyone interested in seeing their church grow more healthily would benefit from reading this. Warmly commended.

Ray Evans, Church Leadership Consultant, FIEC

Where can I learn how the church I attend should be structured and run today? Obviously, if we are biblical Christians, we must turn to the Bible. It is great to get some help, however. The Bible itself teaches us that. These essays will do that. They will help pastors and other serious Christians to think through the fundamental issues that have somehow been forgotten or blurred in people's minds down the years. You may not accept every word they write (they do not necessarily want you to) but you will be driven back to the Bible and what it teaches about church (which they do want) and that can only be for your good. I warmly commend this compact and thought-provoking collection of essays.

Gary Brady, Pastor of Childs Hill Baptist Church, London

In our time the word church has become somewhat inflated: 'church planting', 'church growth', 'church unity', 'church renewal' are all common expressions that can be found across the board of the evangelical movement and the ecumenical world. The problem is: which church? What is the church? Where is the church? The confusion around the word church is massive. I welcome this rich collection of essays defining, illustrating, and commending the biblical model of a 'pure church', the confessing church, the church made of believers who covenant with one another before God. In Italy there is a growing movement of confessional and confessing churches who will benefit from this book. And I am sure that this will also be the case for many more churches around Europe.

Leonardo de Chirico, Pastor of Breccia di Roma Church, Rome, lecturer in historical theology at IFED and Director of the Reformanda Initiative

A prayerful spirit breathes through this book, which is characterised by gentleness, humility, energy, joy – and deep conviction. It is written by eleven seasoned pastors who love God's word and know how to teach it clearly, practically and with helpful illustrations. They believe that the more closely local churches order themselves in God's way, the more clearly they will display the gospel. This can only be done by maintaining the intimate connection that exists between conversion, baptism, church membership and the Lord's Supper. If the biblical teaching of this book is read, pondered and put into practice, our congregations will be holy and happy, growing in godliness to the glory of God.

Stuart Olyott, pastor, author and missionary

Here is a fresh, thoughtful and challenging restatement of a classic Baptist understanding of church order for a new generation. Recently there has been a renewal of thinking about ecclesiology among Reformed or Calvinistic Baptists and this book is a fine example. It is accessible and could be used by study groups in churches with much benefit. While not agreeing with everything in it, the book made me think and appreciate more how the manifold wisdom of God is displayed for his glory in local assemblies of Christians. Take and read.

Ken Brownell, Pastor of ELT Baptist Church, Mile End, London

This excellent little book is proof that independency need not mean isolation! Eleven men – all practitioners, not theorists – join up the dots for a compelling picture of church structure that is biblical, practical and inspirational. Full of real life scenarios, and ideal for stimulating discussion, it clearly answers the charge that 'it doesn't matter how we "do church"'. Jesus promised to build his church; the blended voices in this book give straightforward, helpful insights into the Lord's blueprint.

Phil Heaps, Co-Pastor of Highbury Baptist Church, London

Pure
Church

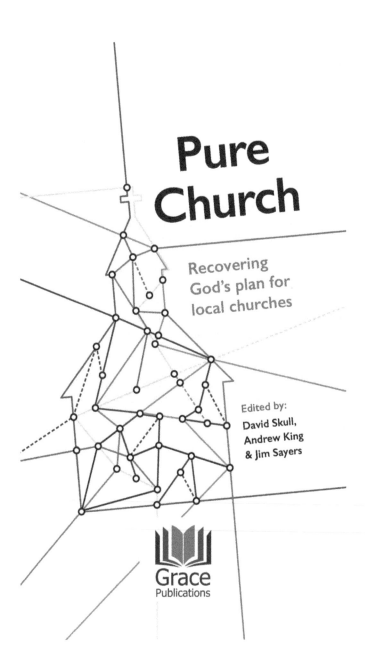

Pure
Church

Recovering
God's plan for
local churches

Edited by:
David Skull,
Andrew King
& Jim Sayers

Grace
Publications

Grace Publications Trust
www.gracepublications.co.uk

First published in Great Britain by Grace Publications Trust in 2018
This revised and updated edition published 2022

Cover design by Pete Barnsley (CreativeHoot.com)

ISBN: 978-1-912154-40-1

Printed and bound in Great Britain by Clays Ltd, Elcograf S.p.A.

1 3 5 7 10 8 6 4 2

The reason I left you in Crete was that you might put in order what was left unfinished and appoint elders in every town, as I directed you.

Titus 1:5

Everything in gospel order

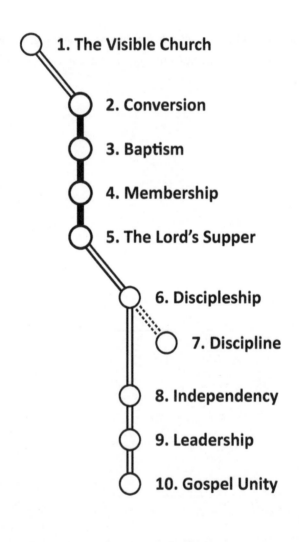

1. The Visible Church

2. Conversion

3. Baptism

4. Membership

5. The Lord's Supper

6. Discipleship

7. Discipline

8. Independency

9. Leadership

10. Gospel Unity

Contents

Preface

David Skull

Back in 2016 a group of pastors got together to ask the question: have Grace Baptist churches had their day? Most of us were serving in Grace Baptist churches; some were from other churches but had similar convictions. All of us were based in the United Kingdom.

So why would we need to ask this question? Some members of the UK evangelical constituency have not even heard of Grace Baptist churches. We have no denominational structure, no bishops or directors. We are independent churches often working in regional associations.

Others have caricatured Grace Baptist churches. 'Aren't you stuck in the 1950s?' 'Aren't you just a bit, well, "strict"?' Some have dismissed us as culturally irrelevant, suggesting that it's harder to join a Grace Baptist church than it is to get into heaven! 'Surely it's unloving to restrict the Lord's Table to baptised believers?'

Have Grace Baptist churches had their day? What is a Grace Baptist church anyway? So we gathered.

We invited a couple of speakers. First, John Benton, retired

Pastor of Grace Church Guildford, reminded us that Grace Baptist churches stand for seven key things:

1. Evangelical truth.
2. A reformed understanding of salvation.
3. The independency of church order. Churches are responsible directly to Christ.
4. A converted membership.
5. Believers baptised into the church.
6. A disciplined Lord's Supper.
7. A Holy Spirit enabled ministry – leadership called and equipped by the Spirit.

Many other churches hold to a number of these things. Grace Baptist churches hold to all seven of them. We shouldn't dismiss these principles. The Bible teaches how we should order our churches, and these distinctives are just what local churches need as we face the future. We need to recapture these principles and reform our churches, not slide into pragmatism.

Second, Bobby Jamieson, Assistant Pastor at Capitol Hill Baptist Church, Washington DC, showed the biblical connection between conversion, baptism, membership and the Lord's Supper. Why have so many churches – even Grace Baptist churches – forgotten this link?

We talked openly, deepened our friendship and respect for one another, prayed and planned. The result was a renewed resolve to order our churches in God's way for his glory, the good of his people and the salvation of lost sinners. We're thankful to Jonathan Worsley, Matt Benton and Luke Jenner who worked on the #TitusOneFive Statement (which for some time was lovingly nicknamed The ERGO Statement – Encouraging the Recovery of Gospel Order). The text of the statement forms the framework for *Pure Church*. It is set out at the beginning of the book, and each clause forms the basis for a chapter.

A writing group was begun. Other writers were added and a year later we met again to share our draft chapters, receive feedback and finally produce this book.

We're excited by this project. We believe in what we have written and long to practise it more faithfully and see it taken up by other churches. We hope it will help you to understand where Grace Baptist churches are coming from and where by God's grace we want them to go. We also hope it will stimulate you to think through how you order your own church. You don't need the label 'Grace Baptist' to see the crucial connection between conversion, baptism, membership and the Lord's Supper. You might not agree with every position we take, but we commend our approach to you as we believe it is a coherent whole.

We are grateful to Grace Publications for being willing to publish this. We are thankful to those who have given us the time to write and encouraged us. Thank you to John and Ann Benton, who took the time to read the manuscript and give us constructive feedback, and to Jonathan Leeman, who did the same from across the pond. Finally, we want this book to be a beginning of a wider conversation in the UK and beyond. We intend to publish more, exploring areas that we have had to cover rather briefly here. We hope that this will stimulate lots of discussion in local churches, leading them to a healthier life and witness for the glory of God. Above everything else, we long to see a movement of churches where the focus is on our glorious Christ, and on living out the life of the local church as he intended.

The #TitusOneFive Statement

Reaffirming the biblical connection between conversion, baptism, church membership and the Lord's Supper

Local churches should be like cities set on hills (Matt. 5:14): gospel communities made up of those saved by the grace of God, recreated by him, and displaying to the watching world the breaking in of God's kingdom of love, righteousness and joy. We want to equip churches to have a biblical vision of this reality, so that the light of Christ might not only be proclaimed, but seen ever more brightly in our generation.

We believe that the biblical elements of a 'gospel order' (conversion, baptism, church membership and the Lord's Supper), ministered lovingly and correctly, together reveal these spiritual realities, and hence become the framework in which a gospel community can thrive.

Doctrinally, we take an evangelical stance as set out in the historic reformed Baptist confessions, and in addition we hold to the following beliefs and practices relating to gospel order:

1.   We believe that the universal church is the body of which Christ is the head, to which all who are saved belong, and that it is made visible in local churches – organised gatherings of Christians – who are:

     i.   united by a statement of faith which expresses the doctrines believed by the church, which are often highlighted, and agreed by every believer who comes into church membership;

     ii.   fed and shaped by the ministry of the word as the focus of their life together in Christ as a gathered church, aided by the gospel signs of baptism and communion.

2.   We believe that a Christian is someone who has been genuinely converted by God. Conversion is radical, and occurs when God gives life to spiritually dead people. It is evidenced in the gifts of personal faith in Jesus Christ, repentance from sin and a changed life of growing obedience and holiness.

3.   We believe that baptism is:

     i.   a local church's act of affirming and portraying a converted person's union with Christ by immersing him or her in water;

     ii.   a converted person's act of publicly committing him or herself to Christ and his people, thereby uniting them to the church and marking them off from the world;

     iii. the act which commences a converted person's membership of a local church.

4.   We believe that anyone wishing to join a local church should be given opportunity to understand the

responsibilities and joys of church membership, and thus agree to the church's statement of faith and the values that govern their life together (perhaps evidenced by the signing of a church covenant). Admission to membership can then occur, after:

i.   the church has affirmed the candidate's profession of faith, evidenced by an explanation of their conversion and the gospel;

ii. the candidate has been baptised as a believer.

5. We believe that the Lord's Supper is:

i.   a local church's act of communing with Christ and each other, and of commemorating Christ's death by partaking of bread and wine;

ii. a converted, baptised person's act of receiving Christ's benefits and renewing his or her commitment to Christ and his people;

iii. Christ's ongoing means of binding the members of a local church together as one body and marking it off from the world;

iv. for baptised members of local churches, whether members of the church where the Supper is being celebrated, or visitors in good standing at another gospel church.

6. We believe that each local church should be characterised by a shared life of discipleship. As all the members are equipped, they should be encouraged to use their gifts to serve others in various works of

ministry and prayer. Together, each local church is to grow in holiness as Christ's bride and in witness as his ambassadors to the watching world. Local church life is to be a growing display of heaven on earth.

7. We believe that church discipline is a provision of Christ for the protection of the honour of his name in a local church. This removal from church membership, and withholding of the Lord's Supper, may become necessary against any church member whose life or doctrine renders their profession of faith in Christ incredible. It is used after much pastoral care, and in order that the offender might be brought back to repentance and faith, and afterwards gladly readmitted to church membership.

8. We believe that each local church has final authority to admit and dismiss members, appoint and remove leaders, and establish the doctrinal and moral standards of the church. These processes should be implemented at regular church members' meetings.

9. We believe that each local church should be led, taught, and prayed over by a plurality of godly and suitably gifted elders, as defined in the Pastoral Epistles, and served by similarly godly deacons, who, for the sake of unity, and for the upholding of the ministry of the word, are to care for particular needs arising in the life of the church.

10. We believe that meaningful fellowship between local churches exists where there is evident faithfulness to the gospel, and that for the sake of displaying unity churches should look to foster good relationships with all other gospel-preaching churches within their locality.

We present these principles in a spirit of submission to the word of God, in acknowledgement of our need of ongoing reform by the Spirit, and in hope of the promotion of warm gospel unity among many.

Soli Deo Gloria.

Introduction

John Benton

Church can be the beauty or the beast. When it's good there is no joy to compare with it. When it's bad – and there are many reasons why it can be – it breaks your heart.

By church, we mean the congregation of God's people united together in the Lord Jesus Christ. The purpose of this book is to show the way for local churches to fulfil what they were designed to do and become holy and happy congregations, growing in godliness to the glory of God.

When a church is functioning as it is meant to, something beautiful happens which nothing else on earth can match. We meet with God. In Spirit and truth, we meet with him in all his glory, grace and wonder.

The famous answer to the first question in the Westminster Shorter Catechism concerning the purpose of human existence rightly tells us that 'the chief end of man is to glorify God and to enjoy him forever.' At church this happens – can happen. It is not the only place it happens, but it is meant to be the primary place. It is beautiful – wonderful beyond telling. We hear from God. We worship and glorify him. We feel a deep satisfaction in our hearts that we have been engaged in our 'chief end' – the purpose for which we were made.

The New Testament describes what we might call the church's divine encounter, in various ways.

The suburbs of heaven

The writer to the Hebrews contrasts the experience of Old Testament Israel with the thrill of the church, by insisting that through the blood of Jesus, already we are in the suburbs of heaven and have come to Mount Zion, to God, to the heavenly Jerusalem, and to the joyful worship of a myriad of angels and the spirits of righteous people made perfect.

The apostle Paul imagines an unconverted outsider coming into a meeting of the gathered church in Corinth, and being convicted of their sins, 'so they will fall down and worship God, exclaiming, "God is really among you!"' (1 Cor. 14:25).[1] God himself is in church.

The apostle John says the same thing in Revelation. The seven letters are written to 'the angels of the seven churches' (Rev. 1:20). 'Don't you usually find angels in heaven? What are they doing in church?' we ask. As he goes on to describe the worship of heaven he speaks of twenty-four elders around God's throne. Again we enquire, 'Don't you usually find elders in churches? What are they doing in heaven?' What John is doing is deliberately blurring the lines between heaven and earth. He is telling us that this happens in church!

---

1 Scripture quotations in this chapter are NIV.

The Lord Jesus himself says it most simply. He tells us: 'Whatever you bind on earth will be bound in heaven, and whatever you loose on earth will be loosed in heaven ... For where two or three gather in my name, there am I with them' (Matt. 18:18, 20). So it is, that a local church can be the most beautiful place on earth. We say with the psalmist, 'How lovely is your dwelling place, LORD Almighty!' (Ps. 84:1).

Churches that please God

We want that profound experience for our churches. We want churches to know the awesome excitement, not just of an accomplished music group or a masterful pulpit presentation, but of the saving presence of God. So we must ask, 'What can we do to make a local church function more clearly as God intended it to? How should churches be ordered so as to please God? What is the best structure?' In other words, we have to ask about ecclesiology.

Historically, evangelicals have shied away from asking too many questions about church. This has been for a number of different reasons – sometimes good-hearted, but always wrong-headed. Here are some classic misplaced arguments.

'Church is a secondary issue'

It is true that church is not the gospel. In that sense it is secondary. But because something is secondary does not mean that it is unimportant and can be shelved. It can, in a way of thinking, be secondary and yet absolutely crucial. We could argue, for example, that the brakes are a secondary item for a car. Surely it is the engine and the wheels and the steering which matter. They actually make the vehicle move and get you where you want to go. But to jump to the conclusion that therefore a car doesn't need brakes, or that we can let the brakes fall into disrepair, means that we will be heading for a crash. Secondary – yes. Unimportant – definitely not!

'The Bible isn't clear on church'

Some Christians seem to have the idea that, though the gospel is clear in Scripture, much else is not. They would say that, apart from a very scanty framework, God has left it up to us to decide how to run his churches. This idea usually comes from good people whose sole aim is the personal salvation of individuals. They have the attitude that as long as we get people into heaven that is all that matters. Thus they tend to have quite a low view of the church. But the Lord does not have such a view. His church is his holy temple, his beloved bride. He could not be more concerned about how his church functions, is organised and is cared for. With their 'personal-salvation-is-all-that-matters' mindset, the eyes of these dear Christians have been blinkered against the fact that ecclesiological concerns are found on almost every page of the New Testament. Would it not be surprising, to say the least, if God, who from eternity has loved and predestined his people and who gave his own Son for their salvation and who gives his Spirit for their sanctification, is content for his church to get along as a DIY, lashed together, ramshackle entity?

'Ecclesiology is divisive'

A concern for the unity of local churches should be in every Christian's heart. It is this proper concern for unity which frequently underlies the arguments in favour of shelving questions about how churches are meant to be organised. Evangelicalism is very much out of fashion in current Western society. Faithful, conservative churches take a lot of flak from the media and many other segments of society. So the argument is that we must stick together as God's people and minimise our differences. Indeed we must hang in with each other and seek to help one another. But a unity which comes about through neglecting or avoiding what Scripture says is hardly what Paul has in mind when he explains that we will grow up into the unity of Christ as we speak the truth in love. The truth about the church is important. It is lovingly seeking and speaking the truth, not avoiding it, that brings about a well-founded unity.

'Being too definite can be off-putting'

Imagine a small church which is eager to attract extra members. Along comes a new family. They begin to attend regularly. They are impressed by the faithful preaching of God's word and the children love the Sunday School. The little church is full of hope they will join. But it turns out that they are from a different church background, with a different way of doing things. Wouldn't it be better not to be so definite about church, be more flexible, and somehow try to accommodate their wishes so they can join? Being too definite about how the church is run might put them off. We sympathise very much with this situation. Certainly some kind of church membership classes where questions can be asked and the church's position explained from Scripture might help. But we can all surely see the absurdity of changing our principles in order to accommodate different people. Suppose you do change the church rules to suit them. What happens when another couple turn up of yet another persuasion? The church will be all over the place. Adopting such a policy will drive a church to a lowest common denominator approach to church and away from Scripture, which is bound to lead to more problems later. We must follow principles not people. Ultimately, the church belongs not to us but to Christ. We must treat people graciously and with patience, but we must be faithful to what we believe the Lord Jesus has revealed in *his* word about *his* church.

'Love is all that matters'

We understand this sentiment. Without love the church loses all its beauty and becomes a beast. There is a supreme need for Christ-like love in local churches. The new commandment of the Lord Jesus to his disciples was that they 'love one another as I have loved you' (John. 13:34). The apostle Paul warns us in the most eloquent but devastating terms: 'If I can fathom all mysteries and all knowledge ... but have not love, I am nothing' (1 Cor. 13:2). So we have to acknowledge that even the truths about the church declared and explained in this book will be of no help without love. Applied without charity and kindness they will ruin churches rather than renovate them. Of course, that is the case. But this is not an either/or situation. The 'love is all that matters' argument presents a false dichotomy. The New Testament wants love in the church, but it also wants truth. We need both, not one or the other.

These arguments and others like them have held sway in evangelicalism for long enough. They won't wash. It is time to look at Scripture afresh and be ready to embrace what the Holy Spirit has to teach us about the way local churches ought to operate.

The sharp church

The local church is God's means of reaching out to a lost world. It is the instrument for playing the winsome, arresting, life-turning tune of the gospel to those only accustomed to the death march of a world on its way to the grave and to hell. It is God's scalpel for cutting out the cancer of sin and restoring people to spiritual health in Christ for everlasting life.

The following chapters seek to spell out the New Testament's teaching on the local church. They will show us how the church is to be a loving community, growing in holiness and to be contrasted with the world. The church should be the shop-window for the gospel of Christ. Local churches should happily proclaim loud and clear, 'Look at us – this is what Christ can do!'

When we neglect ecclesiology, God's scalpel becomes a blunt instrument. We no longer make the people of the world feel embarrassed by the emptiness and superficiality of their lives. We often wonder why the church seems to have lost its cutting edge in the twenty-first century. Could it be because churches have become too relaxed, and no longer disciple and care for their members so as to become vibrant communities of Christ-like people whose lives challenge our society with their joy and purity? Could it be that the way many churches are run does not lead Christians to see their Christianity as much more than a Sunday hobby? Could it be that our churches are not providing the heaven-bound community and deep sense of Christian identity that is needed in these days? Could it be that we have lost the weight of glory?

As the apostles' teaching on the church is explored and put into practice, our churches will be given a gospel edge. Individuals will be honed. Churches will be sharpened for God, the surgeon's, use.

The joined-up church

Over recent years there has been a growing concern for the health of gospel churches. This is to be applauded wherever it is found. But very often that concern has come down to the introduction of a few new items to the church agenda – a Christian foundations course here or a discipleship course there.

However, the agenda of this book is different. The vision of this book, which we believe is a New Testament vision, is that the whole way a church should be formed, run and led should work for the health of all its members and for the thriving of the church as a community of God's people. It is a church with an intentional mindset throughout. It is a church where all the dots are joined-up.

In such a community God's own presence will be manifest. It is not simply about an extra activity or a few extra one-to-one Bible studies bolted on to the existing structure. The church needs to be rethought in a joined-up way, so that the whole organisation and organic life of the church works for building up God's people to his glory.

In his book *The Kingdom of God and the Glory of the Cross*, Patrick Schreiner picks up the biblical picture of God's kingdom as a growing tree. It is strong. It is fruitful. People find shelter and shade under its branches. In a word they find life. He says this: 'Power is not about coercion; it is about structures for flourishing. God created the tree of life out of his power so that Adam and Eve could flourish as human beings, but they turned to the forbidden tree.'[2]

A church ought to be structured so as to make its members thrive. A church which patterns the whole of its life on the premise that, under God and through Christ, it is to be the means by which God's people are to flourish, will be a community which brings people back to the tree of life. It will lead people back into the presence of God.

It is the collective aim of the authors of this book that churches will be shaped by Scripture to grow strong and true. Every local church could be a beauty not a beast.

---

2   Patrick Schreiner, *The Kingdom of God and the Glory of the Cross* (Crossway, 2018), 19.

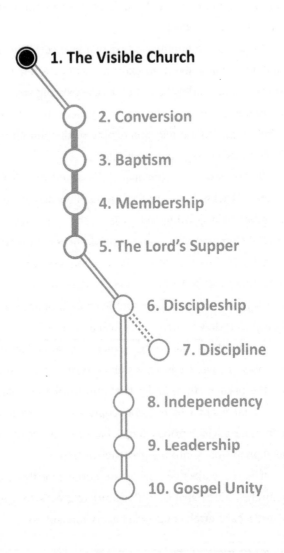

1. The Visible Church

2. Conversion

3. Baptism

4. Membership

5. The Lord's Supper

6. Discipleship

7. Discipline

8. Independency

9. Leadership

10. Gospel Unity

1. The Visible Church

The community the gospel makes

Jim Sayers

1. We *believe that the universal church is the body of which Christ is the head, to which all who are saved belong, and that it is made visible in local churches – organised gatherings of Christians – who are:*

    i. *united by a statement of faith which expresses the doctrines believed by the church, which are often highlighted, and agreed by every believer who comes into church membership;*

    ii. *fed and shaped by the ministry of the word as the focus of their life together in Christ as a gathered church, aided by the gospel signs of baptism and communion.*

Gary hasn't found it easy to settle in a church because of his background in the Watchtower movement. He was brought up as a committed Jehovah's Witness, keeping all the requirements of the elders of his Kingdom Hall, who controlled every aspect of his daily life. God finally opened his eyes to see the claims of Jesus as the eternal Son of God through reading 2 Corinthians 5:21. He grasped that he could only become the righteousness of God in him if Jesus is indeed God incarnate.

Leaving his local Kingdom Hall was worse than a divorce, and now he wonders whether he can ever be part of a normal local church. Won't becoming a full member of a church lead him back into the control from which he has only just escaped? Gary's situation is not unusual. When people leave the cults, or even the Roman Catholic Church where it has been particularly authoritarian, they often struggle to commit to anything else. Do Christians really need to become members of a particular local church if their Christian life is going to flourish?

Craig and Gemma drifted into a relationship several years ago. It is hard to say exactly when they set up home together. Both of them had been with several other partners before then, but somehow they seemed to stay together and this time it worked. They bought a house together, then they had a daughter and now they have a baby son as well.

Craig started playing football on Monday nights with a group of Christians. Gemma enjoyed the church toddler club, and God was at work in both of them at the same time. When one of the lads from football was baptised, they both came to church and were deeply moved by what they saw and heard. Craig became a Christian that night, and Gemma a few days later.

Now they're both thinking about baptism, but that raises an issue: they have never been formally committed to anything in their lives. Could they stay on the fringes of the church, get baptised but not be members? Could they come and go as they feel like it, or does being committed members of a local church matter to their spiritual life?

The invisible church

At one level, Gary, Craig and Gemma already belong to the church. They are alive in Christ, and that means that they are part of his body. Christians believe that when someone trusts in Christ alone as Saviour and Lord, they are united to him and therefore part of the universal body of Christ.

Historically, Christians have affirmed the words of the Nicene Creed: 'We believe in one holy catholic and apostolic church.' This is central to our understanding of the church. The church is one, united in Christ as head of his church. The church is to be holy, declared righteous in Christ by justification, and sanctified by the Holy Spirit to live as a distinctive witness to the world (Matt. 5:14-16). It is also to be catholic in the pure sense of the word, united in Christ across national and denominational boundaries with fellow-Christians from every nation under heaven (John 17:20-21; Rev. 7:9-10).

The Nicene Creed also affirms the church as being 'apostolic', that is, built on the foundation of the apostles and prophets, affirming the truth today that they received first from Christ as Lord of his church. The message of the church is the same truth Christ gave to his apostles, fulfilling all that the Old Testament prophets had already spoken, and the church lives or dies by that apostolic message. All true Christians belong to this universal or 'invisible' church, the body of which Christ is the head.

The idea of the invisible church is popular among evangelical Christians because it fits with the ambiguities of a post-modern age, and is easy for us all to identify with. However, the universal or invisible church is made visible in the local church. God's plan for his church is that it should be formed of local groups of believers, each of which is known as a church.

Paul writes 'To the church of God that is in Corinth' (1 Cor. 1:2), one particular and defined church.[1] He also speaks of 'all the churches' (14:33) as local churches which can be separately identified from each other. He uses Old Testament imagery to describe the church in Corinth as a body of Christians. As a local church they are 'God's field, God's building' (3:9), and 'God's temple' (3:16). When they gather, they are 'in church' (14:35) which suggests gathering in some formal way to worship God. They 'come together' (5:4; 14:26) in such a way that everyone knows who belongs to this local body of Christ, and who does not. While in some places in 1 Corinthians Paul does speak of the invisible or universal church (e.g. 10:32; 15:9), for most of the letter he is addressing a local church, a church with boundaries and definition, a church which can be marked out.

---

1 Scripture quotations in this chapter are ESV.

'Doing church'?

When I was a child, on a wet Sunday afternoon we children would gather in the sitting room to 'play chapel.' Either my older brother or I would 'preach', while the other would lead the singing, and our sisters would bustle in and out with dolls that apparently were crying too much! I blush to think of what I might have said as a seven year old; we were acting out a church service as seen superficially through our young eyes.

There is a danger that adults can do something similar, in the sense that we can put on a show that is entertaining. That might be a cool gig in a warehouse with dimmed lights and walls covered with rough cut wood panelling, with a preacher in ripped jeans and a check shirt and beard. It could just as easily be something more traditional, loaded with liturgical language and the right clothing, polished pews and a pipe organ, whether that be Catholic, Anglican or traditional Baptist. Whatever your preference, this can simply be 'doing church' from a human point of view, and the presence and power of God can be absent, though no one realises.

The true local church is something done by God. It is God who brings a church into being through the preaching of his word, and baptism and communion mark those who have been changed by that word and brought to life in Christ as belonging to that church. A local church that preaches the gospel is the most eternity-shaping, heart-breaking, dead-raising, life-giving, heaven-empowered, grace-giving community there can ever be, and it is the centre of God's mission.

To understand why it is that the gospel creates visible local churches, first we need to think about the essentials of that gospel and how denying these doctrines will destroy the local church. Then we need to go a step further and ask: does a gospel church have to be definite about what it believes about itself? Some Christians would say that local churches should be as inclusive as possible when it comes to baptism and communion, and should not be too prescriptive about membership. Grace Baptist churches have taken a more definite position. We will ask whether that is separatist and divisive. Finally, we will look at how this is worked out in the local church as they gather together around the word of God, putting God's truth at the heart of their shared life as the basis of their spiritual health, aided by the two gospel signs of baptism and the Lord's Supper, living out our important calling to be the visible church together.

The gospel – the things of first importance

Paul wrote 1 Corinthians to a church in all sorts of trouble. He covers an immense array of issues, before coming to the elevated climax of the letter in chapter 15, where he gives his clearest summary of the gospel. These are the things of first importance, and we will use them as our framework. Each key doctrine that Paul sets out in the opening verses is essential to the life of a local church. This is the message that brings local churches into existence and sustains their spiritual life. A church will eventually die if it denies any of these key doctrines. They can be summarised under six headings.

The foundation of God's word (vv. 2-3)

Paul preached the gospel to the Corinthians, and they gladly received it, not as Paul's words but as a word from God. 'For I delivered to you as of first importance what I also received' (v. 3). His message was always 'in accordance with the Scriptures.' Paul was a man under authority, a servant of the word, passing on only what he had received as an apostle of Christ sent from God. The message that Paul proclaimed to the Corinthians was 'of first importance'. God's word written is the highest authority in our lives. The message of Christ is unchanging and for all time, and it is contained in all its riches in our completed Scriptures.

When Paul says that 'Christ died for our sins in accordance with the Scriptures' (1 Cor. 15:3) he says something profound about the unity and sufficiency of Scripture. The whole Bible is one book, breathed out by God through human authors, so that Old Testament mysteries have lines of promise that all find their fulfilment in Christ. When Christ died, he fulfilled the whole of Scripture. Therefore, this ultimately rich and dynamic book is the foundation of everything we believe. A gospel church is brought into being by the word of God. Without Holy Scripture there is no message of salvation, for without it God would remain unrevealed and his grace unexplained in all its richness.

Whenever a local church begins to treat the Bible as a book that is dubious in places, reducing it to a book of wisdom among many others, it is in trouble. Yet far too many churches pass by or reject narratives, psalms and prophets that speak of God's justice, or Old Testament law and New Testament letters that deal with male and female roles or sexual morality, and parables and apocalyptic visions that speak of final judgment and hell. A gospel church places itself under Holy Scripture as its final authority, believing that it is breathed out by God the Holy Spirit, that it reveals Christ to us and shows him to be the way to God the Father. We proclaim only what we have received.

The death of Christ for sin (v. 3)

What is the message of the Bible? '...that Christ died for our sins in accordance with the Scriptures' (v. 3). Paul packs so much truth into so few words. The identity of the Christ is the central issue in the heart of Scripture. All the prophets, priests and kings of the Old Testament foreshadowed the Lord's ultimate anointed, the divine, eternal Son. The incarnation of the Son of God tells us both that God is real and gracious, and that sin is serious. Human sin must be punished by a holy God if his justice is to be satisfied, and while the one who is punished must be human, no man or woman is able to fill that role except the man who is God, the Christ. Perhaps the word most loaded with meaning in this verse is the preposition 'for' (Greek *hyper*), because it defines the rich achievement of the cross. Christ died instead of us, as our substitute. Christ did not merely die to identify with us in our sin, or to show sympathy with us in experiencing the curse of death. He died in our place, bearing our punishment for us, paying the ransom price we could not pay, satisfying the wrath of God that we can never satisfy ourselves.

The statement 'Christ died for our sins' is the fulcrum of the church's power. Everything turns on these words. Deny them, and there can be no peace with God. Evade them by suggesting that some weaker understanding of the cross will be an adequate explanation of Jesus and his mission, and you empty the cross of all its power. The two signs given to mark the church, baptism and communion, are each a vivid re-enactment of the one salvation event on which our eternity depends. Jesus purchased the church of God with his own blood (Acts 20:28). This truth brings churches into being all over the world.

The resurrection of Christ as Lord (vv. 4-8)

Paul spends much more time in 1 Corinthians 15 emphasising the resurrection than he does the cross. Why is that? People from both Jewish and pagan backgrounds had little problem with the idea of blood sacrifice. What repulses people in our secular culture was normal to them. What was beyond comprehension was resurrection. Therefore, in verses 4-8 Paul labours the actual, physical nature of the resurrection appearances. The apostles were all witnesses of the risen Christ, and testified that he truly rose from the dead. Indeed, 'he was raised on the third day in accordance with the Scriptures.' The resurrection fulfils all the promises of the Old Testament, that one day the seed of the serpent will finally be crushed. The victory of the risen Christ over death and the curse is then worked out in the rest of the chapter, together with the promise that Christ's resurrection is only the firstfruits. Christians will see the goodness of God in the land of the living and dwell with God in a new creation for ever.

This means that the local church is a community of resurrection. The power that raised Jesus from the dead is at work in us, bringing the spiritually dead to life and giving us the hope of eternal life. We are not to be gatherings of the nostalgic and the despondent. Christ is risen! We are to be communities of hope and power.

The power of grace (v. 10)

Christians are those who are 'being saved' (v. 2) and for whose sins Christ died (v. 3). The human condition is desperate. It is not that God brings us good news in Christ, and tries his best to sell it to us, and we independently decide whether we accept it. The human condition is much worse than that. We are rebels against a holy God, incapable of repenting and believing in our own strength. That is why Paul uses the passive voice in verse 2 – we are *being saved* by God; we are not saving ourselves. Paul was particularly appalled at his own rebellion as an unworthy persecutor of the church. Only grace could explain his salvation. 'But by the grace of God I am what I am, and his grace to me was not in vain.' The grace of God is the source of the church's life. Grace chose us from all eternity, and intervenes in history, both in the incarnation and death of Christ, as well as in the mission of the church. The grace of God is never in vain, because what God resolves to do, his grace always achieves. A nerve of grace runs through history, invincible and unstoppable, bringing life and energy to the spiritually dead, and awakening with goodness and spiritual life those who deserve only God's severity and death. The grace of God brings each local church into existence, and works through that church to send the impulse of God's grace onwards to awaken a dead world. Paul says of his own apostolic mission in verse 10, 'I worked harder than any of them, though it was not I but the grace of God that worked in me.' The grace that brings us to new life is also the grace that equips us to reach a lost world.

Saving faith (vv. 2-3, 11) ·

Paul says that the message of God's grace that came to the Corinthians was a message that 'you received, in which you stand and by which you are being saved, if you hold fast to the word I preached to you – unless you believed in vain ... so we preach and so you believed.' The work of Christ at the cross becomes effective by God's grace as he works in us to empower us to respond. Faith can be described as 'receiving' the gospel in the sense of believing it is true, and of 'standing' in it, that is, grounding our entire life on what Christ has done for us. This shows in a changed life, because what we believe is not just an assent of the mind but an opening of the heart and a submission of the will. We 'hold fast' to the promises of the gospel because they mean everything to us. It is essential to ensure that those who belong to the local church have genuinely trusted in Christ, and live a changed life that gives evidence that they are holding fast to the promises of the gospel. The nature of true repentance and faith is worked out more extensively by Adam Laughton in the next chapter.

The return of Christ (vv. 2, 23-28)

All Paul's affirmations in 1 Corinthians 15 lead up to the main body of his argument, namely that the reality of Christ's resurrection should prepare us for his return. We hold fast to the gospel in the light of that day, when our faith will be vindicated. At his coming, all his enemies will be put under his feet as he sits in final judgment on the human race, and all those who belong to Christ will be eternally saved. Local churches are to keep their eyes fixed on that day, when everyone will be held to account. The realities of eternal punishment motivate us to be urgent in mission. At the same time, local churches are to be 'colonies of heaven', a foretaste of the life of the new creation.

A true confession

These six doctrines Paul sees as truths 'of first importance.' Without them churches die; through them, Christians are brought to new life and churches are brought into being. The truth they proclaim is the gospel that gives life and brings people into the community of a living, local church. Therefore that church has to be clear about the doctrines it believes and proclaims. For this reason, since the early church it has been necessary for churches to define Christian truth in creeds and confessions of faith. While no creed or confession is infallible Holy Scripture, confessions of faith have stood the test of time and have been both a valuable bulwark in refuting heresy and a helpful way of systematising and teaching the truths of Scripture so that Christians can grow in their grasp of Christian truth. Some churches subscribe to a long confession, such as the Westminster Confession or the 1689 Baptist Confession, while many will have something less extensive. Some churches expect only their leaders to sign the church's confession of faith, while they require all those coming into membership to accept it as the church's position, even if they themselves may disagree on one or two points. Others require all who become members to agree to the whole statement of faith, and take the opportunity to read and affirm it publicly together.

Is this requiring too much as the basis of the unity of a local church? Some argue that in a gospel church there should be unity on gospel essentials only, as you might expect among members of a university Christian Union or when inviting speakers to the Keswick Convention. Going beyond that is divisive, they say, and local churches should try to include true Christians from a wide diversity of positions and church backgrounds, minimising the amount of definition needed for a local church to exist. What is the effect of this in practice? It is to blur the boundaries of a local church, to say that the things that mark a local church do not really matter.

Historically, Christians have defined the local church by two marks, the clear and faithful preaching of the word of God, and the right administration of baptism and the Lord's Supper. The word of God brings the church into being and sustains its life, while baptism and the Lord's Supper mark out those who are the members or 'living stones' that make up the 'spiritual house' that is the local church (1 Pet. 2:5). Baptism and the Lord's Supper are Christ's commands (Matt. 28:19; Luke 22:19), the boundary markers he gave to his church. They are an expression of the discipline of belonging to a local church, while the word proclaimed enlivens the life that is shared within this Christian community.

Because they are marks that define the boundaries, a church has to define what it believes about the 'sacraments' of baptism and communion, or 'ordinances' as Baptists have preferred to describe them. If infant baptism and believer's baptism are treated as equally valid in one church, baptism becomes a sign with many and conflicted meanings, something to be chosen by the individual according to their preference rather than being a clear sign practised by that local church. If communion is separated from baptism, it likewise loses its corporate identity as a sign of belonging to the local church, and becomes much more a sign of the invisible church than the disciplined local church. Above all, taking a lowest-common denominator approach to our understanding of church, or even an approach which says two or more contradictory positions can be equally valid, is to say that Scripture cannot be clear on any of these things.

First and second-order doctrines

How do we decide which doctrines should define a local church? Al Mohler has made a helpful distinction in defining what he describes as a 'discipline of theological triage.'[2] Churches have to sort key doctrines into three categories or levels. First-order doctrines are those most central and essential to the Christian faith, such as the six doctrines classified as being 'of first importance' above. These doctrines are essential to salvation, and so they form the basis of our fellowship with all other Christians. A disagreement over these issues cuts to the essence of the gospel.

However, there are second-order issues and third-order issues. Second-order issues are where believing Christians most often disagree, and these disagreements most commonly lead to the boundaries that mark out different visible local churches. That is because churches have to be churches. They have to decide what they believe about how a church operates – who should be baptised, who should take communion, who should lead, how church discipline should operate and so on. Baptists, Presbyterians, Anglicans, Brethren churches and others will disagree on these issues, because we disagree on the marks of the visible church. We want to stand together as Christians on the first-order doctrines, but we recognise that on second-order issues we belong to different churches and respect our differences.

Third-order differences are those that Christians can

---

2 A. N. Mohler, 'A Call for Theological Triage in Christian Maturity', 20 May 2004, https://albertmohler.com [accessed 15/11/21].

disagree on within the local church, because they are not essential to the operation of that church: details of eschatology, the age of the earth, or whether to be teetotal or vegetarian, do not need to be defined by a local church.

So are Grace Baptist churches being unnecessarily divisive and separatist because we believe that baptism as a believer is the sign that brings a Christian into the membership of the visible church, and that the Lord's Supper is an expression of belonging to that local church? We don't think so. Baptism and communion are not signs that can be fudged. They both have a rich meaning that is in danger of being seriously eroded in a post-modern age. They tell us that the visible local church is important, and that it is defined and marked by these two signs. Baptism is a gospel sign that speaks of God's work begun in bringing someone to new life and into the church, and the Lord's Supper is a gospel sign that reminds us that we continue the Christian life through communion with Christ as part of his visible church. Baptism and the Lord's Supper are signs that must be given their gospel importance in the life of the local church if they are to reach their full meaning and significance.

The gathered church

Many Christians want a church to be like their supermarket. They are looking for what pleases them, ticks their boxes and feels reassuringly comfy, especially if the church is large enough to slip in and out of without being noticed or getting involved. Middle-class churches defy community, shared life and belonging, with their rows of chairs, professional presentation, paid staff and 'event management' approach to gathering. But God has given us two most powerful signs, baptism and the Lord's Supper, to explain what the church is about. Baptism requires us to admit what we were, and to testify to what God has made us by his grace, and to be marked by the church in God's name as belonging to his church. The Lord's Supper is also known as communion because it unites us together in our Saviour and Lord, reminding us that we are sinners communing together in a local church, in continual need of redemption and committed to caring for one another.

The consumer Christian, who prefers to pick and choose, cruising from church to church, never comes to know the intimacy and communion of a living, caring local church. Some Christians are giving up on church altogether, perhaps because they have been damaged by an experience of church in the past, or because they buy into the idea that we can 'live free' of any church and just be what we are in Christ, getting our spiritual food online. But Christ called us to be part of his church, and in the New Testament the local church is always a gathered church.

The biblical pattern is for a local church to meet together for worship as an expression of commitment to God and to one another (Heb. 10:25). The word of God flows through the gathered life of the church, because we believe that that is how God speaks to us and nurtures our spiritual lives. It is because Christians believe that the Bible is from God, and centred upon Christ, and every word and context breathed out by the Holy Spirit, that we place it at the heart of our church life (2 Tim. 3:16-4:5).

We want the preaching of the word to be central to our gatherings, because it is the message of God's word that awakens the dead and feeds the living. The breadth and richness of Scripture's content also provides a diet that will keep any preacher feeding his congregation for a lifetime without ever exhausting its supply (1 Tim. 4:13-16).

We want all that we sing and pray in a church gathering to be overflowing with the words of Scripture so as to reinforce its message in our lives (Col. 3:16). We make sure that God's word is being read by every Christian in the church to feed their spiritual growth, and the leaders apply it to every pastoral situation they deal with.

A living gospel church should be a continual cycle of the word of God bringing people to life, baptising them into the life of the local church where they are discipled, encouraged and cared for, and sending them out with the same word to the world to tell others the good news of Jesus.

Conclusion

People like Gary, Craig and Gemma struggle with the idea of being committed members of a local church. That is mainly because they have each had a problem with organised institutions and rigid rules. Gary thought he had left all that when he escaped from a cult. Craig and Gemma, like a significant minority of British couples, had decided they didn't need the institution of marriage to be happy. So is the local church a dead institution that will only deprive us of our joy and stifle our spiritual life? Not if it is working as God intended! The local church should be the visible outworking of the gospel. God, through his word, brings people into new life in Christ, and brings them together in local churches. The gospel we believe and proclaim should shape our worship, empower our shared discipleship, drive our motivation for mission, fuel our prayers and give us confidence for the future. At the same time, baptism and the Lord's Supper should mark the saved from the unsaved as God-ordained gospel signs, not to be seen as the frowning border guards of a city under siege, but rather as the winsome signposts to the visible and shared life that is a healthy, gathered, gospel church.

Questions for discussion

1. 'Surely I can be a Christian without becoming a member of a local church?' How would you answer this question?
2. What evidence is there that the universal church is made visible in local churches? (1 Cor. 1:2; 3:16; 5:4)
3. Read 1 Corinthians 15:1-11. What first-order truths (essential to salvation) must a church hold to?
4. What issues do the whole church need to agree on to function as a church? What beliefs can Christians disagree on and still belong to the same church?
5. How has your understanding of the local church developed from reading this chapter? Commit these things to the Lord in prayer and thank God for your church as it makes the universal church visible.

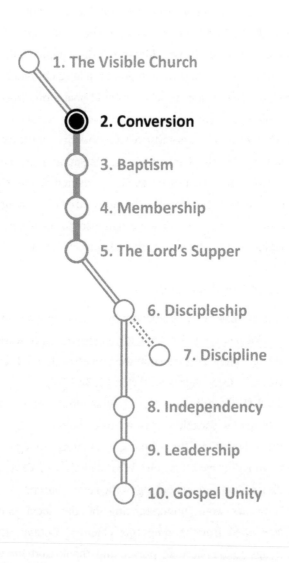

1. The Visible Church

2. **Conversion**

3. Baptism

4. Membership

5. The Lord's Supper

6. Discipleship

7. Discipline

8. Independency

9. Leadership

10. Gospel Unity

2. Conversion

The radical work only God can do

Adam Laughton

2. *We believe that a Christian is someone who has been
   genuinely converted by God. Conversion is radical,
   and occurs when God gives life to spiritually dead
   people. It is evidenced in the gifts of personal faith in
   Jesus Christ, repentance from sin and a changed life of
   growing obedience and holiness.*

Night of the living dead?

How 'dead' must a person be, before we register them as truly
dead? What process might be needed to restore them back
to genuine life? Don't worry; we've not suddenly entered the
frightening realm of horror or science fiction. It's just that the
theme of Christian conversion raises issues of profound and
lasting change. In fact, our view of conversion impacts our
views on prayer, evangelism, church and assurance – to name
but a few areas! In short, we must be clear about conversion.

So what is conversion? How does it happen and how
profound is it? Is conversion simply a choice, or a change

of allegiance, much like a decision to join a political party or community group? Or is it much more radical? We need to turn to the Bible for some answers.

> And you were dead in the trespasses and sins in which you once walked, following the course of this world, following the prince of the power of the air, the spirit that is now at work in the sons of disobedience – among whom we all once lived in the passions of our flesh, carrying out the desires of the body and the mind, and were by nature children of wrath, like the rest of mankind. (Eph. 2:1-3)[1]

The short answer is this: Christian conversion is profoundly radical because the human condition is profoundly desperate. Outside of Jesus Christ, every single human being on our planet is 'dead in trespasses and sins.' Of course, people are alive: they eat, move, think, speak, laugh and cry. They go to work, hug their children and watch TV. But at the same time, they are spiritually dead.

What's more, they are content with being spiritually dead. Having no desire to know God, they are busy 'living' in the 'passions of their flesh, carrying out the desires of body and mind.' Now there are some pretty nasty people around, but not everyone is a paedophile or war criminal. Truth is, most people are fairly 'humdrum' human beings. So how can Paul describe them in such awful terms? Put simply, their lives are lives of disobedience to God; the direction of their lives is firmly set against God's will and wishes. They are unwilling and

---

1   Scripture quotations in this chapter are ESV.

unable to love God, turn to God or obey God. So conversion cannot be something we do to ourselves. It must be something that only God can do. It requires nothing less than giving new life to dead sinners. Jesus teaches the same thing.

> Truly, truly, I say to you, unless one is born again he cannot see the kingdom of God ... unless one is born of water and the Spirit, he cannot enter the kingdom of God ... You must be born again. (John 3:3, 5, 7)

Jesus was speaking to a respectable religious teacher called Nicodemus. If we were trying to find anyone spiritually qualified to follow God, surely it would be somebody like Nicodemus? Yet Jesus is clear: our state is so desperate that nothing short of a spiritual new birth can help us.[2] Jesus' phrase 'water and spirit' is a reference to God's promises preached by the prophet Ezekiel.[3] When Nicodemus expresses surprise at Jesus' words, Jesus challenges Nicodemus, 'Are you the teacher of Israel and yet do not know these things?' (John 3:10). If Nicodemus had reflected on his Old Testament for a moment, he would realise that even God's people, Israel,

---

2 Also referred to as 'regeneration.' As the word implies, we need a new spiritual life to be generated within us.

3 'I will take you from the nations and gather you from all the countries and bring you into your own land. I will sprinkle clean water on you, and you shall be clean from all your uncleannesses, and from all your idols I will cleanse you. And I will give you a new heart, and a new spirit I will put within you. And I will remove the heart of stone from your flesh and give you a heart of flesh. And I will put my Spirit within you, and cause you to walk in my statutes and be careful to obey my rules' (Ezek. 36:24-27).

needed a radical experience of new birth before they could know the living God! Jesus is not creating a new doctrine when he says, 'You must be born again!'

Rescue of the living dead!

Why would God even want to help us, given that our lives are opposed to everything he stands for and loves? Even if God did want to help, how would he do it? Prepare to be amazed:

> But God, being rich in mercy, because of the great love with which he loved us, even when we were dead in our trespasses, made us alive together with Christ – by grace you have been saved – and raised us up with him and seated us with him in the heavenly places in Christ Jesus, so that in the coming ages he might show the immeasurable riches of his grace in kindness towards us in Christ Jesus. For by grace you have been saved through faith. And this is not your own doing; it is the gift of God, not a result of works, so that no one may boast. For we are his workmanship, created in Christ Jesus for good works, which God prepared beforehand, that we should walk in them. (Eph. 2:4-10)

Why are people converted? Simply because of God's love and grace. Paul is straining to express just how incredible God's love truly is. God is 'rich in mercy' even to hell-deserving 'god-haters' like you and me. His ultimate purpose is that in eternity, he might show to the universe the 'immeasurable riches of his grace in kindness towards us!' (Eph. 2:7). The God of the Bible is a loving, kind, gracious, wonderful Saviour God! We don't deserve any of his love, yet he pours it out on us in spades!

How are people converted? God 'makes us alive together with Christ' (Eph. 2:5). In God's wonderful plan of salvation, sinners are given new birth through being united spiritually with the Lord Jesus Christ. This 'union' with Christ is something worked in our hearts by the Holy Spirit, and as we are united to Jesus Christ, we receive all the fruits of his saving work. In a very real and profound sense, we share in the life, death, resurrection and ascension of Christ. And so, one consequence of sharing in Christ's resurrection is that we receive new spiritual life.

Implication: radical, biblical conversions produce radical, biblical local churches

A church that grasps the profound nature of true conversion cannot remain unchanged. For example:

- How do we see church membership? We are now alive in Christ, in a world of dead sinners. Of course, we are thrilled to see non-Christians at our public meetings. But local church membership can never be a mix of Christians and non-Christians. How can it? How can death and life be united in the same body? Or how can we imagine that our unsaved children are 'part of Christ's body' unless and until they are themselves converted?

- How do we see non-Christians? Our hearts go out to them in pity and love. Churches that understand conversion are places where non-Christians find a genuinely warm welcome and love.

- How do we see evangelism? Can you or I raise the dead? We know the answer. No matter how impressive our preachers, how effective our bridge-building or how clear our evangelism courses, we cannot convert a single person. If God does not act, nothing happens! Churches that grasp the biblical reality of conversion *must* by definition be churches that consistently and earnestly pray together for the salvation of the lost. A church that does not pray with urgency does not truly understand conversion.

Calling out to the living dead...

Conversion is impossible unless God graciously works in a human heart. So far so good. But having made that point, we also affirm the vital agency of preaching in conversion. For it is by the word of God and the Spirit of God that people are made spiritually alive.

> How then will they call on him in whom they have not believed? And how are they to believe in him of whom they have never heard? And how are they to hear without someone preaching? And how are they to preach unless they are sent? As it is written, 'How beautiful are the feet of those who preach the good news!' But they have not all obeyed the gospel. For Isaiah says, 'Lord, who has believed what he has heard from us?' So faith comes from hearing, and hearing through the word of Christ. (Rom. 10:14-17)[4]

---

4   See also the conversion of the 3000 at Pentecost (Acts 2:37ff), the opening of Lydia's heart (Acts 16:14-15) and Paul's description of his preaching in 1 Thessalonians 1:4-10.

Conversion is not a mystical experience, divorced from content or knowledge. It is not just a change of direction, brought about by a vision of 'god' or an ecstatic worship experience. It is wrought in a person's heart as they hear the gospel message. It is a mysterious work of the Holy Spirit, who takes the gospel message and empowers it with life-giving power, so that when a person hears it, they are made alive spiritually. This 'effective' or 'effectual' call makes all the difference. Suddenly it all makes sense! It grips their mind, heart and will. They willingly respond to the gospel message truly for the first time.

Implication: churches that want conversions will be 'preaching churches'

Preaching of the gospel through all and any means will be at the heart of every local church's strategy to win the lost. Of course, the apostolic approach to preaching was much more varied and multi-faceted than just one man standing in a pulpit twice on Sundays.[5] However we get that message out, a lost world needs to hear the gospel message with clarity and urgency. As we evangelise, our hearers must be in no doubt that we have an authoritative message about their eternal destiny. Healthy local churches will always remain fully committed to preaching.

---

5   For a summary of the varied evangelistic approaches of the early church, see Arthur B. Rutledge, 'Evangelistic Methods in Acts', *Southwestern Journal of Theology*, Vol 17 (Fall 1974).

First cry of the new-born!

Every conversion is unique, because every person is unique, created by a God of infinite creativity. For some, conversion happens at a clear moment in time, perhaps in a 'crisis' experience. For others, conversion may be a gradual experience. A person may say, 'At that point in time, I was not a Christian, yet now I am a Christian; but when it happened, I'm not sure.' This diversity of experience needs to be reflected in our pastoral care. We should not demand that people conform to a narrow, prescribed 'process' before we accept their testimony as genuine.

However, at the same time, conversion is the same for everyone, consisting of two essential and united elements: repentance from sin and faith in the Lord Jesus Christ.

> The time is fulfilled, and the kingdom of God is at hand; repent and believe in the good news. (Mark 1:15)

> If you confess with your mouth that Jesus is Lord and believe in your heart that God raised him from the dead, you will be saved. (Rom. 10:9)[6]

Repentance and faith are two sides of the same coin; the two essential ingredients that together constitute conversion in its precise sense. We need to remember that they belong together, but we shall look at each in turn.

---

6 The early church preached repentance and faith, for example: Acts 2:38; 3:19; 16:31; 26:20.

Repentance

The New Testament understanding of repentance is to 'turn around' or 'to change one's mind'.[7] Repentance involves a change of direction that affects the whole person: mind, emotions and will. It begins with a true understanding of biblical truth about God and leads to a conviction of our guilt before God. This creates an inner resolve to reject sin and live a life of obedience to God:

> For godly grief produces a repentance that leads to salvation without regret, whereas worldly grief produces death. For see what earnestness this godly grief has produced in you, but also what eagerness to clear yourselves. What indignation, what fear, what longing, what zeal, what punishment! At every point you have proved yourselves innocent in the matter. (2 Cor. 7:10-11)

True repentance has clearly affected the entire personality of these Corinthian believers. Their godly grief has led them to earnestly seek to be 'cleared', i.e. they wish to have their blotted records wiped clean before God and one another.

As the name implies, 'godly sorrow' results from an awareness of Almighty God, his holiness and judgment. It recognises our sin firstly as an offence against God, and only afterwards as the offending or harming of others. Worldly sorrow, in contrast, focuses primarily on the effects

---

7   Several words express this idea in the New Testament, including: *metanoia* (meaning 'change of mind, or repentance') and *epistrepho* (meaning 'turn, turn around, change, be converted'). See Verlyn D. Verbrugge (ed.), *New International Dictionary of New Testament Theology* (Zondervan, 2003), 367.

or consequences of our actions. By its very nature, worldly sorrow is self-centred.

It is clearly possible for people to feel 'sorry' for the bad things they do, yet not truly repent. People may regret the consequences of their actions. They may even acknowledge in some sense that they have offended and disappointed God, yet not truly repent.

So imagine Charlie – he's just got back to his car to discover a parking warden about to issue him with a parking ticket! He is alarmed – he doesn't want to pay a hefty fee. He takes action – he pleads with the traffic warden ('I'm only 5 minutes late! I'm leaving now!' etc.). But in the end, the traffic warden is fair in issuing him a ticket. Afterwards however, Charlie is complaining to his wife about the whole sorry event: 'It's so unfair! He's such a jobs-worth! Why couldn't he let me off? I'm so cross!' It's all about Charlie, isn't it? Although he was sorry that he had been caught, Charlie was not truly repentant about his bad parking, nor did he truly believe that he deserved a fine. That's worldly sorrow.

David Garland helpfully explains in his commentary:

> Godly grief differs from a worldly grief in several ways ... Worldly grief is caused by the loss or denial of something we want for ourselves. It is self-centred ... By contrast, a wonderful example of godly grief was penned by the converted slave trader, John Newton, who came to recognise and confess his wretchedness and blindness in the hymn, 'Amazing Grace.'[8]

---

8 David E. Garland, *New American Commentary on 2 Corinthians* (B&H Publishers, 1999), 355.

Faith

At its heart, 'to have faith' means to believe or trust in someone or something. A person must not only turn from their sin, but at the same time, they must believe or trust in the Lord Jesus Christ to save them.

Even in everyday life, faith can be nuanced. We 'trust' all manner of people and things in our daily lives, yet the depth of our trust varies enormously, as does the amount we think about the person we are trusting. From eating a meal that someone has cooked for us, to sitting on a chair, making an online payment to a company we've not used before, to saying 'YES!' to a marriage proposal. All of these involve faith, yet even these few examples demonstrate that faith can operate on several levels.

So what does genuine saving faith consist of? The Bible explains that genuine saving faith requires several things to be present: knowledge, assent and personal trust.[9, 8]

True faith needs knowledge. Faith is not a leap into the dark – quite the opposite! A person must know facts about God,

9   The Latin terms of *Noticia, Assensus* and *Fiduca* were probably first coined by the reformer Phillip Melancthon, in his 1521 theological treatise, *Loci Communes Theologici*. Since then, it has been a common three-fold understanding of faith used by many of the Puritans and even contemporary reformed writers.

10   These three elements are hinted at in 1 Thessalonians 2:13: 'And we also thank God constantly for this, that when you received the word of God [knowledge], which you heard from us, you accepted it not as the word of men [assent] but as what it really is, the word of God, which is at work in you believers [trust].'

sin, Jesus and the gospel, before they can believe or trust them (Rom. 10:14). But knowing the truth is not enough, for a person may dislike or reject these facts, especially since all people are sinners, desperate to maintain their own personal sovereignty in the face of a God they would rather ignore or avoid.[11]

True faith needs my assent. Assent happens when a person agrees with the truth, believes it to be true and even approves of the truth as a good thing. This is clearly a vital step forward, but it's still not enough. I may know and believe that the life ring you've just thrown me may save me from drowning – but I need to grab that life ring or else I'm sunk! That final act of 'grabbing' is what we may term 'personal trust' in the Lord Jesus Christ.

True faith needs my personal, active trust in Jesus Christ. Christianity is located in the person and work of the Lord Jesus Christ. He is the Saviour and the Lord. True saving faith must involve a personal commitment and engagement in the living Lord Jesus Christ as Saviour and Lord.

> For God so loved the world, that he gave his only Son, that whoever believes in him should not perish but have eternal life. (John 3:16)

It is striking to note that to be saved, a person must 'believe in' Jesus Christ. It is not simply enough to believe Jesus (i.e. believe he is trustworthy, or that what he says is true),

---

11 So, sinners may know what God wants, yet approve of those who rebel against him (Rom. 1:32) and the demons know and believe that God is real, and they tremble, but their 'faith' clearly has not saved them (James 2:19).

but rather we must place our faith in Jesus himself – in his person, in his works, and in his promises. True saving faith is seen when a person personally entrusts themselves into the hands of the Saviour. They stake their eternal destiny on Jesus' promises as expressed in the gospel. They give up their efforts of self-salvation, and fling themselves into the arms of Jesus Christ to forgive them, save them and bring them ultimately into heaven. Leon Morris expresses it in these words: 'Faith, for John, is an activity which takes men right out of themselves and makes them one with Christ.'[12]

Blondin was a famous tightrope walker, who amazed the crowds by walking across the raging river that plunged over the top of the Niagara Falls. For one of his shows, he was planning to push a wheelbarrow across the rope, from one side to the other. He asked the assembled crowd, 'Do you believe that I can do this?' One young man cried out, 'I know you can, Sir! You are the famous Blondin!' Upon hearing this exuberant young man's praise, Blondin looked at him, and replied, 'In that case, will you please sit in the wheelbarrow?' Do you see the point? If my faith is real, I will completely entrust myself (and my eternal salvation) into the hands of the Lord Jesus Christ. To change the metaphor, I must put all my (spiritual) eggs in *his* basket! I trust *him* alone to save me.

Saving faith is so much more than 'deciding to follow Jesus' or 'praying a sinner's prayer.' While it can be expressed simply

12   Leon Morris, *The Gospel According to John* (Eerdmans, 1971), 336.

as 'Believe on the Lord Jesus Christ', that word 'believe' must infuse the entire personality of a person, so that they entrust themselves fully into Jesus' hands.

Genuine repentance and faith are inseparable

It should be apparent by now that repentance and faith are two inseparable sides of the same coin. Repentance would only be genuine if it included a true trust in Jesus Christ as Saviour and Lord. And faith would only be genuine if it included a turning from self-reliance and sinfulness.

Implication: we must challenge people to 'Repent and believe the gospel' (Mark 1:15)

Only a vigorous, heart-searching evangelism does justice to the doctrine of conversion:

- Does our evangelism seek to do justice to the profound depths of change that repentance and faith demand of a dead sinner? Or do we simply call on people to 'let Jesus into their lives' as though they were welcoming home a lost friend?

- Dare we presume that doing a few evangelistic courses will automatically lead to some people 'deciding for Jesus'?

- Do we imagine that simply by answering people's objections and questions, we will argue them into the faith?

We must challenge people as lovingly as we are able to realise that they are dead in their sins, and under God's judgment. We must call on them to seek God with all their heart, to repent of their shameful self-reliance and rejection of God and to cry out to the Lord Jesus Christ today, in the hope and expectation that Christ will save all who call on him.

Fruits of conversion: a new life in union with Christ

Lisa and Lara began attending a local gospel church around the same time. Both grasped the gospel and expressed a growing desire to become Christians. Over one summer, both of them publicly repented of their sin and professed faith in Jesus Christ as their Lord and Saviour. After a few months, both of them were baptised in the church, to the obvious delight of all.

Fast forward two years. Lisa is still meeting regularly with the Lord's people, and has grown in her Christian faith. She's had some ups and downs, including a traumatic spell in hospital, but she gives every indication of still walking in a relationship with Jesus. Sadly, however, Lara no longer attends. After her initial joy of baptism, she began to struggle with doubts. Soon afterwards, she lost her job and became disheartened. After a while, her attendance grew erratic and she began spending more time in activities outside of her church fellowship. She's also now involved sexually with a non-Christian. Currently she does not attend, and if you asked her, she says, 'I'm still a believer, but I don't feel the need to come to church. God understands.'

What has happened? What are we to make of these two professing Christians? Would it be harsh to say, 'Lisa was clearly converted, but Lara's conversion must have been false'? Was the church foolish to baptise them both? Should they not have checked them out for longer?

Only God can see our hearts, so we should not be quick to make shallow judgments of other people. Yet at the same time, the Bible is clear that conversion leads to a changed life. It also teaches that repentance and faith are not a single act that happens once, when we are converted. Rather they are lifelong attitudes that we exhibit as part of our daily, healthy Christian walk with God. 'And forgive us our sins, as we forgive those who sin against us' is a daily prayer for Christians. In other words, Christians sin and need forgiveness every day, and so we pray to God our Father to forgive us anew.

However, true conversion will lead to a life that moves away from sin. The reason for this is found in our union with Christ, as the apostle John explains:

> No one who abides in him keeps on sinning; no one who keeps on sinning has either seen him or known him ... No one born of God makes a practice of sinning, for God's seed abides in him, and he cannot keep on sinning because he has been born of God. (1 John 3:6, 9)[13]

Clearly John is not saying that Christians are sinless. Earlier

---

13 See also 1 John 2:4-6, where John says, '... whoever says he abides in him [i.e. Jesus] ought to walk in the same way in which he walked.'

in his letter, John says, 'If we say we have no sin, we deceive ourselves' (1 John 1:8). Christians are still sinners. John is saying that the Christian life is one of moving away from sin, and of overcoming sinful habits and practices. As the Spirit of God works in a Christian's heart and life, that person finds strength and grace to grow in holiness and obedience. So if a person's lifestyle is characterised by regular, unrepented disobedience, it is unlikely that they are truly converted.

Notice John's use of phrases like 'in him' and 'abiding'. This is the language of union. Put simply, when we are born again and converted, we are united to Christ by the Holy Spirit. It is this union with Christ that forms the context and the basis for all our Christian life. This spiritual union brings us into a living and essential relationship with Jesus Christ. All that belongs to Christ is now ours, and all that was once ours is taken by Christ and dealt with.[14]

It is impossible to overstate the importance of the doctrine of union with Christ:

- We are initially united with Christ in regeneration (Eph. 2:4-5, 10)

- We appropriate and live out this union with Jesus through faith (Gal. 2:20; Eph. 3:16-17)

- We are justified in union with Christ (1 Cor. 1:30; 2 Cor. 5:21; Phil. 3:8-9)

---

14 See Paul's words again: 'God ... made us alive together with Christ ... raised us up in him and seated us with him in the heavenly places in Christ Jesus ... For we are his workmanship, created in Christ Jesus for good works ...' (Eph. 2:5, 6, 10).

- We are sanctified through union with Christ (1 Cor. 1:30; John 15:4-5; Eph. 4:16; 2 Cor. 5:17)

- We persevere in the life of faith in union with Christ (John 10:27-28; Rom. 8:38-39)

No wonder, then, that John Murray wrote, 'Union with Christ ... is the central truth of the whole doctrine of salvation ... it is not simply a phase of the application of redemption, it underlies every aspect of redemption.'[15] It is because we are in Christ, united to Christ, abiding in Christ, that our new lives begin to look more and more like Christ's life. Hence, a truly converted person must begin to live a changed life.

Implication: biblical conversion leads to biblical discipleship

This surely means that we should expect every professing Christian in a local church to be growing in grace, love and knowledge of Jesus Christ. As Jesus expresses it:

> I am the vine, you are the branches. Whoever abides in me and I in him, he it is that bears much fruit, for apart from me, you can do nothing. (John 15:5)

What are we to make of that grumpy professing Christian, who remains in such a sour state for years? What about the member whose attendance is patchy for no good reason, yet who always seems to find time for weekend breaks or any one of a thousand other hobbies? Our view of conversion, surely,

---

15 John Murray, *Redemption* (Eerdmans, 1955), 201, 205.

must lead us to challenge, lovingly, what true spiritual work is being done in their hearts. If there is life, there must be signs of spiritual fruit, especially growth in grace, love and knowledge of Jesus Christ (2 Pet. 3:18).

Final implication: union with Christ means union with his body, the church

Now we come to the rub: if I belong to Jesus and Jesus belongs to me, then I belong to Christ's body, his church. Christ's people are my people, and I am theirs. If I am united to Christ, and other Christians who live close to me are also united to Christ, then I will become united to them too. That means I will meet with them regularly, join myself to them publicly in membership and commit myself to them (and they to me) in a loving covenant as we seek to serve the Lord and one another. Failure to do so is a contradiction of our union to Christ.

It is an oft repeated maxim amongst mainstream evangelicals that membership is not that important. A preacher was once challenged, 'Surely I can be a Christian without being a member of a local church. I can attend church, but why do I need to become a member?' The preacher, half in jest, said, 'Of course! But while we're on the subject, let me show you this severed finger that I keep in a matchbox in my pocket!' After the shock, the preacher explained. 'You and I are members of the same body. That has to mean something. We are spiritually united in a living union to Jesus Christ and one another. If you just attend church, without being united to it, you are like this severed finger. You may be close to me, but you are not joined to me. Pretty soon, your spiritual life will wither and rot."[16]

Conclusion

In the end, our understanding of biblical conversion affects almost every aspect of local church life. If our local churches grasp the truth about conversion (or perhaps better, if we are grasped by the Bible's teaching on conversion!) then it will surely transform us for the better.

Let me close with a question and a hope.

How is the world to see the life of God? Of course, they will see it in the changed lives of dead sinners converted to life. But I want to say more than that. For these Christians, born again by the power of God and united to Christ, will express that union and life by living in loving union with one another. It is through the united gospel witness of local church communities that the life-giving reality of the gospel is seen most clearly. As John writes:

> In this is love, not that we have loved God but that he loved us and sent his Son to be the propitiation for our sins. Beloved, if God so loved us, we also ought to love one another. No one has ever seen God; if we love one another, God abides in us and his love is perfected in us. (1 John 4:10-12)

If our churches are filled with truly converted and transformed people, then the evangelism battle is already half won! May

---

16 I am grateful to Ali McLachlan of Grace Baptist Partnership, Scotland, for this illustration.

God pour out his Spirit on our church communities, our prayer meetings and our preaching!

Questions for discussion

1. Read Ephesians 2:1-10. How does Paul describe the radical change in his readers?
2. How does this doctrine of conversion shape local church membership?
3. What evidence should a church look for before welcoming someone into its membership? (Mark 1:15; Rom. 10:9; 2 Cor. 7:10-11; 1 Thess. 2:13)
4. Name your fellow church members and then spend some time thanking God for his rich mercy and great love in making you all alive together with Christ. (Eph. 2:4-5)

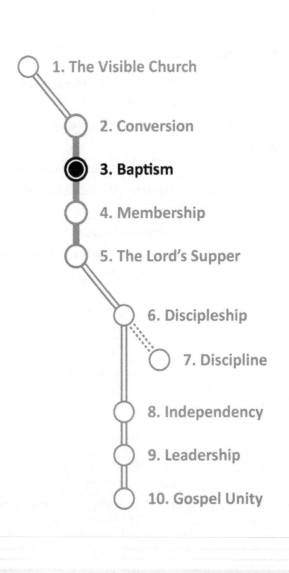

1. The Visible Church

2. Conversion

3. Baptism

4. Membership

5. The Lord's Supper

6. Discipleship

7. Discipline

8. Independency

9. Leadership

10. Gospel Unity

3. Baptism

The first sign of community membership

David Skull

3. *We believe that baptism is:*
   i. *a local church's act of affirming and portraying a converted person's union with Christ by immersing him or her in water;*
   ii. *a converted person's act of publicly committing him or herself to Christ and his people, thereby uniting them to the church and marking them off from the world;*
   iii. *the act which commences a converted person's membership of a local church.*

A couple of years ago Grace Church Guildford kindly gave me a sabbatical. I'm not sure who needed the break more – them or me. Anyway, our family took the chance to head over to America for a study break and a holiday. Everything in America is big ... and on first impression upbeat and encouraging. This includes the Baptists! We ended up staying on the campus of the Southern Baptist Theological Seminary in Louisville, Kentucky. It was big and we loved it. The students and staff were welcoming and I even managed to sneak into some lectures. But what I really loved was the library. Every day of my study leave I would grab my Starbucks coffee – yes, there was even a Starbucks on campus! – and just sit in that big place of learning to read and think. I read books on Baptist church history. I even found books detailing the history of my church back at home. Grace Church Guildford's history goes back at least to the first half of the seventeenth century and possibly earlier. There is something surreal yet soothing about discovering your own church's history sitting in a library 4000 miles from home! I felt I was rediscovering my roots. I came away affirmed and convinced that a Baptist understanding of the church was biblical and right not just for the past three centuries but for twenty-first-century Britain as well.

Why did it take a period of study leave in a big Baptist seminary to bring this about? Back in the UK, Baptists are not big. Our churches are often small and struggling. Sometimes we wonder if our practices are more out of tradition than biblical conviction. Others, who don't seem to think much or care much about the minutiae of baptism, membership and the Lord's Supper, are just getting on with sharing the gospel and leaving the other bits to work themselves out, and it looks like it's working.

Surely those old Baptist ways are hindering not helping the spread of the gospel? After all, when a church denies good gospel people membership because they haven't been baptised in the proper way, aren't they out of step? Don't we have bigger fish to fry?

It's true: baptism can be *over-stressed*, especially in Baptist churches. I remember attending a baptismal service when I was younger that left me feeling frustrated and uncomfortable. There were unbelieving guests there to support their friend who was getting baptised. What an opportunity for the gospel! Unfortunately, the preacher couldn't see beyond the baptism to the gospel it portrayed. His message was mainly focused on the mode not on the Messiah. Even as a young person I found myself inwardly shouting 'Preach Christ – not the water.'

However, if we *under-stress* baptism and forget its link to conversion, church membership and the Lord's Supper, we are in danger of watering down the church and the very gospel we are rightly committed to proclaiming. I think most of us are in more danger of doing this today and our churches are weaker as a result. Baptism really is a big fish for the church.

In this chapter I want to affirm the importance of Baptist baptism for the health and life of the local church. It is not my intention to write a polemic against reformed paedobaptism, although I want to be clear from the outset that I do not consider the baptism of infants to be baptism. Others have recently written excellent defences of this view from the Bible with a spirit of warmth and generosity to those who oppose them. I commend them to you.[1] Instead I want to

---

1 See Bruce Ware 'Believer's Baptism View' in David F. Wright (eds), *Baptism* (IVP, 2009); Thomas D. Schreiner and Shawn D. Wright (eds), *Believer's Baptism* (B&H Academic, 2006); David Kingdon, *Children of Abraham* (Grace Publications, 2021).

encourage pastors and elders of Baptist churches and other baptistic free churches to stick with Christ and his apostles on baptism.

You don't need a sabbatical in the States to get this. You just need your Bible and a willingness to follow God's recipe.

Here's how the rest of this chapter will go: after defining baptism I want us to see that it is a practice commanded by the risen Jesus himself, not something to be taken lightly by any church or any Christian. Then we'll think about who should be involved in baptism, what it means and how it should be practised. I'll then finish with some implications for the life and witness of churches in Britain today.

Are you with me? Don't let this fish get away. It's big.

Defining baptism

According to our statement, we believe that baptism is first of all a local church's act of affirming and portraying a converted person's union with Christ. This is done by immersing him or her in water. Second, it is the act of a converted person, publicly committing him or herself to Christ and his people, thereby uniting themselves to the church and marking them off from the world. Finally, baptism is the act which commences a converted person's membership of a local church. This is not delayed to a later stage.

We're leaning heavily here on our American friend Bobby Jamieson. He's written two very helpful books on the subject which we recommend to you for further reading.[2] Let's work with this definition as we look at the Bible together.

Commissioned by Christ

Firstly, let's remember that baptising is Christ's command for his disciple-making church:

> And Jesus came and said to them, 'All authority in heaven and on earth has been given to me. Go therefore and make disciples of all nations, baptizing them in the name of the Father and of the Son and of the Holy Spirit, teaching them to observe all that I have commanded you. And behold, I am with you always, to the end of the age.' (Matt. 28:18-20)[3]

I hope you want to be part of a disciple-making church! But how do we do it? Well, to obey Jesus' command to go and make disciples, two things must happen. First, new disciples must be *baptised*, and then new disciples must also be *taught* all that Christ has himself taught.

The act of baptism is not essential to salvation (see Acts 16:31; Rom. 10:9; 1 Cor. 1:13-17) but it is not unimportant. It is commanded by Christ and his command must be obeyed. We cannot be missional, evangelistic and discipling if we're not also baptising.

Lucy began attending church in February. A Christian friend had already invited her to watch and discuss the *Life*

2 Bobby Jamieson, *Going Public* (B&H Academic, 2015); Bobby Jamieson, *Understanding Baptism* (B&H Academic, 2016).

3 Scripture quotations in this chapter are ESV.

Explored course after their sports training and when invited to church Lucy came and just kept coming. God was clearly working in her life – we could all see it. In April she heard the preacher explain Acts 2:38, 'Repent and be baptized every one of you in the name of Jesus Christ for the forgiveness of your sins, and you will receive the gift of the Holy Spirit' – and she did! Everyone could see what was happening to Lucy. Her friends couldn't understand it but the church was overjoyed. In obedience to Jesus we soon baptised her and made sure she was quickly meeting up with an older Christian sister to get grounded in the faith.

Let me encourage you ... and, if you're like me, give you a bit of a loving nudge. Baptism is part of the Great Commission and therefore commanded by Christ for the church. Sometimes we find ourselves saying 'Why don't we see many baptisms any more?', when we should really be asking, 'How can we be going and making disciples more?' I need that nudge, don't you?

Here's the great encouragement behind the commission. The church is not alone. All authority has been given to our risen Lord Jesus and he has promised to be with us always.

So let's get going. For Lucy's friend, 'going' meant living for Jesus at the sports club where they trained. Don't wait for them to come in. Encourage your church to be a going church, and, as people come to faith in Christ, baptise them when they do.

The 'who' of baptism

On the surface this looks like a silly thing to say. Surely the 'who' of baptism is the one getting baptised! After all it is well known that baptism is an individual's response to the command 'repent and be baptised' (Acts 2:38). But look again at our definition. There are two 'who's in baptism: We believe that baptism is *a local church's act* and *a converted person's act*. Baptism requires both a church to baptise and a converted person – a believer – to be baptised. So there are two 'who's in baptism. Let's think first about the 'who' of the church.

Who does the baptising?

Usually it is the pastor or elders of the church who are in the water with the one getting baptised. But they do so as representatives of the whole church. It is the church that has the responsibility to baptise.

To understand this let's see how Jesus' Great Commission to make disciples and baptise them builds on his previous statements on binding and loosing in Matthew's gospel. Follow the trail with me from Matthew 28 back to Matthew 16 and 18.

> Go therefore and make disciples of all nations, baptizing them in the name of the Father and of the Son and of the Holy Spirit. (Matt. 28:19)

> If your brother sins against you, go and tell him his fault, between you and him alone. If he listens to you, you have gained your brother. But if he does not listen, take one or two others along

with you, that every charge may be established by the evidence of two or three witnesses. If he refuses to listen to them, tell it to the church. And if he refuses to listen even to the church, let him be to you as a Gentile and a tax collector. Truly, I say to you, whatever you bind on earth shall be bound in heaven, and whatever you loose on earth shall be loosed in heaven. Again I say to you, if two of you agree on earth about anything they ask, it will be done for them by my Father in heaven. For where two or three are gathered in my name, there am I among them. (Matt. 18:15-20)

And I tell you, you are Peter, and on this rock I will build my church, and the gates of hell shall not prevail against it. I will give you the keys of the kingdom of heaven, and whatever you bind on earth shall be bound in heaven, and whatever you loose on earth shall be loosed in heaven. (Matt. 16:18-19)

Jonathan Leeman has helpfully shown the connection between these passages.[4] In Matthew 16, Jesus gives Peter the power of the keys of the kingdom of heaven. This means that Peter (who has just confessed Jesus' true identity) and the other apostles have heaven's authority to affirm or reject (bind or loose) citizens of the kingdom of heaven (Matt. 16:18-19). But look how the same language is used in chapter 18. According to Jesus, this 'power of the keys' is the work of the local church – not just the apostles. So when the problem of a persistently unrepentant sinner is told to *the church*, the church can use this same authority to treat them as a pagan sinner. Jesus uses

4   Jonathan Leeman, *The Church and the Surprising Offence of God's Love* (Crossway/9Marks, 2010), 177-195.

the same language of binding and loosing in 18:18 as in 16:19. We must conclude therefore that the church has the same heavenly authority to affirm or reject citizens of the kingdom.

Now Matthew 28:18-20 completes the picture. Heaven's authority here is given by Jesus to his disciples (and by implication the church) not just to affirm and reject who Jesus' disciples are but to actually go and make them, by baptising and teaching. So when a new disciple is baptised, *the church* affirms and accepts them on Christ's behalf.[5] Baptism is the church's act and the church speaks on behalf of heaven.[6]

Wow! What a responsibility the local church has, delegated from the Lord Jesus himself! When a church baptises someone, they give earthly affirmation that this is truly a disciple made in heaven. We dare not treat this responsibility lightly.

What does this look like in practice? At Grace Church we invite all those who wish to join the church to some membership classes. They get the chance to hear what the church believes and how it functions. We try to be clear from the very outset that baptism is not an optional extra but biblically required for church membership. An elder (often with their wife) will then meet with an applicant. We ask them how they have come to repentance and faith in Christ, what they understand the gospel to be and what difference their faith in Christ makes to

---

5   See Jamieson, *Going Public*, 88-89; Jonathan Leeman, *Church Membership* (Crossway/9Marks, 2012), 61, 62, 89.

6   I take Philip's baptism of the Ethiopian eunuch to be a surprising exception but not the rule. Presumably he was then to return to begin the Ethiopian church!

their lives on a day to day basis. At the end of the day though, the decision to baptise an individual and add them to the membership is a church decision not an eldership one. So after a report back to the eldership and with their approval the applicant's name is shared with the church members. Over three weeks the members are able to feed back to the elders any comments as to their suitability for membership. At a members' meeting the elders will then share their testimony and after some feedback from the gathered church we vote to baptise (if they have not already been baptised) and to accept them into membership. After baptism, the new member is officially welcomed in at the next Lord's Supper.

Does this sound a bit ponderous? It's not meant to be. We're just trying to take seriously the whole church's responsibility to bind/baptise true disciples of Jesus. How do you do it? Who's your 'who' when it comes to baptising? It should be the church.

Who gets baptised?

The other 'who' of baptism is the one the church is baptising. Baptism is also *a converted person's act* of publicly committing him or herself to Christ and his people, thereby uniting them to the church and marking them off from the world.

We've already seen in Matthew 28:19 that disciple-making and baptising go hand in hand. So those who are not disciples should not be baptised by the church. We see many examples of believer's-only baptism in Acts.[7] For example on the day of Pentecost, it is those who 'repent' and 'receive his word' that are baptised:

> Now when they heard this they were cut to the heart, and said to Peter and the rest of the apostles, 'Brothers, what shall we do?' And Peter said to them, '*Repent* and *be baptized* every one of you in the name of Jesus Christ for the forgiveness of your sins, and you will receive the gift of the Holy Spirit. For the promise is for you and for your children and for all who are far off, everyone whom the Lord our God calls to himself.' And with many other words he bore witness and continued to exhort them, saying, 'Save yourselves from this crooked generation.' So those who *received his word* were *baptized*, and there were added that day about three thousand souls. (Acts 2:37-41; italics added)

This is the consistent pattern in Acts. Only believers are baptised.[8] This means that unless there is evidence of faith and repentance there should be no baptism. Surely, we don't have unbelievers queuing up to join our churches in the twenty-first century? Well maybe not, but there does need to be discernment. Young people can be caught up with positive

---

7   Bruce Ware has listed all the many examples from Acts, 'noting (by the use of italics) the relation in each text between prior belief and subsequent baptism.' See Ware, 'Believer's Baptism View', in *Baptism*, 25-27.

8   'In the experience of becoming a Christian, five integrally interrelated components took place at the same time, usually on the same day: repentance, faith, confession, receiving the gift of the Holy Spirit, and baptism.' Robert H. Stein, 'Baptism and becoming a Christian in the New Testament', *SBJT*, 2 (1998), 6-17.

peer pressure; others want to please Christian parents but may not be the Lord's. Some even apply for membership when they are really just seeking a spouse. It has been known!

Conversion and water baptism go together. But how can we tell if the applicant is really a disciple of Christ? The church must look for evidence of faith and repentance and the new life of the Spirit in those who wish to be baptised. Erroll Hulse is helpful here by pointing us to 1 John:

> Every candidate should pass the three basic tests which John repeats over and over again in his first epistle. He must pass *the moral test*, that is holiness of life (1 John 3:9) ... *the social test*, giving evidence of genuine love for the Christian family (1 John 3:14, 15) ... *the doctrinal test* (1 John 4:2) in that he possesses a personal, living and clear perception that Jesus Christ is the Son of God.[9]

If an application 'fails' the conversion test then it provides a wonderful opportunity to work through the gospel with that person and to pray for the Lord to bring them to a living relationship with him through the gospel.

If we only baptise disciples, that also means that dear Christian brothers and sisters who have been 'baptised' as infants in churches which believe and practise paedobaptism have not been baptised at all. It is not enough to say that they have been baptised according to their own conscience. Only believers can be baptised and to be watered before faith,

---

9   Erroll Hulse, 'The Implications of Baptism', in *Local Church Practice* (Carey Publications, 1978), 52. See also John W. R. Stott, *The Letters of John* (IVP, 2003), 57.

repentance and receiving the Holy Spirit is not baptism and serves only to empty baptism of its true significance. This may lead to some difficult conversations but it will not be good for the individual or our local church in the long run to allow an unbaptised believer into the membership.

What does baptism signify?[10]

First, *we now belong to the Triune God.* Jesus speaks of 'baptizing them in the name of the Father and of the Son and of the Holy Spirit' (Matt. 28:19). So believers are publicly connected with the true and living God.

Second, *we have been united with Christ in his death, burial and resurrection.* Let's see this from Romans 6. 'Are we to continue in sin that grace may abound?' Paul asks (Rom. 6:1). No way! But see how he backs up his answer. Christians are not to continue in sin because we have died to sin. There has been a decisive break with the power of sin in our lives. But how does he argue his case? He appeals to ... wait for it ... our common experience of baptism!

> Do you not know that all of us who have been baptized into Christ Jesus were baptized into his death? We were buried therefore with him by baptism into death, in order that, just as Christ was raised from the dead by the glory of the Father, we too might walk in newness of life. (Rom. 6:3-4)

Paul could have said 'Do you not know that all of us who have

---

10 The points in this section are taken from Gregg R. Allison, *Sojourners and Strangers* (Crossway, 2012), 353-7.

been *united to Christ Jesus by faith were united into his death...*' but he didn't. He chose to appeal to their baptism. Now let's be clear, water baptism itself does not unite us to Christ – we are united to Christ by faith, and baptism is the sign of this union. But such is the link between believing and being baptised that Paul is happy to say that we have 'been baptised into Christ'. So baptism signifies and affirms that we really are united spiritually with Christ, in his death, burial and resurrection. It is in this way that we have died to the power of sin and are now alive to God.

Isn't that encouraging! When I became a Christian, I died to sin. The sinful life is no longer the life for me. I know that because I was baptised into Christ as a Christian.

Now this is important. For this argument to be relevant for all believers, Paul must be presuming that all believers had been baptised, otherwise his appeal to baptism would have no explanatory power. Baptism symbolises our union with Christ in his death, burial and resurrection. Every Christian should be able to nod their head and remember their baptism.

Third, baptism also reminds us that *we have been cleansed from sin*, and who doesn't need that reminder? When Paul recounted his conversion experience in Acts 22:16, he remembered that Ananias urged him to '... rise and be baptized and *wash away your sins*, calling on [Jesus'] name.' So baptism signifies a spiritual cleansing.[11] As we are washed physically,

---

11 See also 1 Corinthians 6:11; Ephesians 5:26; Titus 3:5 where Paul probably alludes to baptism. For more, see Schreiner, 'Baptism in the Epistles', in *Believer's Baptism*, 83-86.

we picture that we have been washed spiritually. 'I'm clean', we should all be able to say. 'I've been baptised!'

Baptism also speaks of our *escape from divine judgment.* In 1 Peter 3 the apostle makes a connection between the eight people saved through water in Noah's ark and his readers' own baptism. Peter makes it clear that we're not saved by water baptism itself, but the act is 'an appeal to God for a good conscience, through the resurrection of Jesus Christ' (1 Pet. 3:21). But we can be sure we will be saved by looking back to our baptism and all that it signifies.

Finally, baptism doesn't just signify spiritual blessings. It actually does something as well. *Baptism incorporates us into the new covenant community, the church.* This is the normal pattern in the book of Acts.[12] On the day of Pentecost 'those who received his word were baptized, and *there were added that day* about three thousand souls.' This involved devoting 'themselves to the apostles' teaching and the fellowship, to the breaking of bread and the prayers' (Acts 2:41-42). Baptism begins our life in the local church. It is the front door to the house of God. All who belong pass through baptism. So as a believer, a true disciple of Christ, is baptised, they signify both that they belong to Christ already and that from that moment on they also belong to Christ's body on earth, the local church.

---

12 Philip's baptism of the Ethiopian eunuch is an exception in the book of Acts (8:26-40). 'On the front lines of gospel expansion, baptism immediately follows an individual's profession, and the church follows as soon as there are multiple Christians to constitute it' (Jamieson, *Going Public,* 101).

> I belong to God – Father, Son and Holy Spirit.
>
> I've died to sin.
>
> I'm clean.
>
> I will be saved.
>
> I belong to the church.
>
> I've been baptised!

How should a church baptise?

Having thought through who baptises, who is baptised and what it signifies, the meaning of baptism fits well with its mode. Our definition speaks of immersing someone in water.

This is the meaning of the verb *baptise* which is used consistently in the New Testament for believer's baptism. Both the descriptions of Jesus' baptism (Matt. 3:16) and the Ethiopian's baptism (Acts 8:39) imply they were immersed.[13]

Baptism as immersion also fits nicely with the various New Testament meanings of baptism that we have just highlighted. Our union with Christ in his death, burial and resurrection (Rom. 6:3-4; Col. 2:11-12) is portrayed by going down in the water to death and burial, then up again to resurrection life. Our total cleansing from sin is shown by our bath from head to toe. Our assurance of rescue from judgment through the resurrection of Christ (1 Pet. 1:21) is pictured as we rise from the waters.

Sprinkling or pouring just doesn't adequately portray the

---

13   Ware, 'Believer's Baptism View', in *Baptism*, 21-22.

gospel in the way that baptism is intended to.[14] We should submerge, immerse, dip, dunk when we baptise. It is in the meaning of the word.

What does this look like in practice? In my experience, British Baptist churches tend to baptise by pivoting a believer back on their heels. We lay them down below the water into their watery coffin before raising them up to life. Others have different approaches. While visiting different churches in America we witnessed the baptisms of new believers in a large evangelical Baptist church. The baptistery was smaller and deeper. The believer held onto the pastor's arm and was lowered down and up, like bicep curls at the gym! Around the world, some baptise in barrels. Others still go down to the river. No doubt there are many differences in the practice of baptism, but it should be by submersion and by the church.

Recap

Let's remind ourselves of what we have seen about baptism so far. We've defined baptism as a local church's act of affirming and portraying a converted person's union with Christ by immersing him or her in water. It is also a converted person's act of publicly committing him or herself to Christ and his people, thereby uniting them to the church and marking them off from the world. Finally, it is the act which commences a

---

14 The sending of the Holy Spirit is both a baptism and a pouring (Acts 1:5; 2:17), so the disciples were both immersed in and soaked in the Spirit. These are different pictures of one extraordinary event, but baptism is still immersion.

converted person's membership of a local church.

We then saw the link between baptism and Christ's Great Commission to the church (Matt. 28:19). While the act of baptism does not save, it is a command of Christ to be obeyed.

Despite our focus on the individual choosing to be baptised, we've seen that there are two 'who's in baptism. Firstly, the church is given authority to baptise and so affirm a believer's union with Christ by faith. Secondly, the believer is baptised and publicly commits himself or herself to Christ and his church. Those who have not believed, repented, confessed or received the gift of the Spirit should not be baptised. They have not been united to Christ by faith.

We've seen various meanings of baptism in the New Testament. The main one is to symbolise a believer's spiritual union with Christ in his death, burial and resurrection. Baptism not only affirms that this has happened; it also portrays this to the watching world. That is why baptism should be by immersion, not sprinkling or pouring, as the word itself indicates.

Application

So what does this mean for churches today?

Let's not separate what God has joined together: conversion and baptism

Paul could not have argued as he did in Romans 6 if the church in Rome had accepted unbaptised members, or if this was the practice in any of the early churches. When someone believes, the next step in their discipleship should be baptism. It is the church's job to make disciples. Immersing them is part of the job description, and what a joy it is!

Do we teach this in our evangelistic courses or our one-to-one meet-ups with seekers? Do we regularly mention this from the front as we appeal to unbelievers present in our gatherings to repent and believe? Is baptism just the next step for a really keen Christian that they may in time get round to when they feel the moment is right? No way! Baptism is the first step for every Christian. Without it, a church cannot affirm that someone really is a Christian in the first place.

Baptism and church membership

Are we in danger of losing the vital connection between baptism and membership of the local church? Or have we even made the link in our churches? By emphasising the 'who' of personal decision, we may well be forgetting the 'who' of the church, and it's to the church that the baptised believer then belongs.

So, if the biblical data has been rightly understood in this chapter, then it means someone cannot be a member of a church without being baptised. Neither should someone be baptised without then belonging to a local church, except in the most unusual circumstances (Acts 8:26-40). Let's not separate what God has joined together. We'll be stronger, healthier and obedient if we do.

Let's be willing to stand out and stand together for Christ

Grace Church Guildford is probably the oldest Baptist church in Surrey, but over the years our story has been one of spiritual decline as well as growth. In the early 1800s the church met in a building known rather quaintly as Charcoal Barn, and the church was in a low state.[15] During this time, two young men were converted and stood before the church. Their names were George Comb and John Andrew Jones. The church affirmed them as disciples of Christ. But before they baptised the two men, the church set to work. It caused quite a stir. What were they doing? They were digging a baptistery in their chapel building. Previous baptisms had been in the river. As the church dug down, neighbours and other churchmen who did not share their convictions came to watch ... and mock. 'What are they doing with such a large hole in Charcoal Barn?' said one. 'Oh,' said the other, 'they are making a large family vault to bury all the Anabaptists in!' Undeterred, the job was done. George Comb and John Andrew Jones were baptised and went on to make quite an impact for the gospel.

Baptism has always been a stand-out sacrament. The world sees that you no longer belong to them; you now belong to Christ and his church on earth. We need the believers of the same calibre as George Comb and John Andrew Jones in our churches. Let's not lower the bar for membership any lower than Jesus does. And let's not be ashamed of baptism.

---

15 Ralph Chambers, *The Strict Baptist Chapels of England*, Vol 1 (Rushden, 1952), 27.

Conclusion

Looking back, I loved my time with the Baptists in America. I loved their upbeat, just do it attitude, whether that was the pastor bicep-curling those believers in the baptistery, or the resources and teachers of that Baptist Seminary. I loved the chance to reconnect with British Baptist history and the doctrine of the church in the library. But here's the encouragement. You don't need a three-month sabbatical to do that. It's all there in your Bible. So with the assurance that the risen Lord Jesus is with us always, let's lead our churches to go and make disciples, baptising them in the name of the Father and the Son and the Holy Spirit. May there be many more baptisms in our generation, whether that be in our baptisteries, swimming pools, ponds, rivers or the sea.

Questions for discussion

1. Is baptism a first-order, second-order or third-order issue for a local church? (Matt. 28:18-20; 1 Cor. 1:13-17)
2. What role does the church take in a believer's baptism?
3. Think about your own baptism. What different things did it signify? (Matt. 28:19; Rom. 6:3-4; Acts 22:16; 1 Pet. 3:21; Acts 2:41-42)
4. Why should baptism be by immersion?
5. How has this chapter deepened your understanding of the relationship between conversion, baptism and the church?

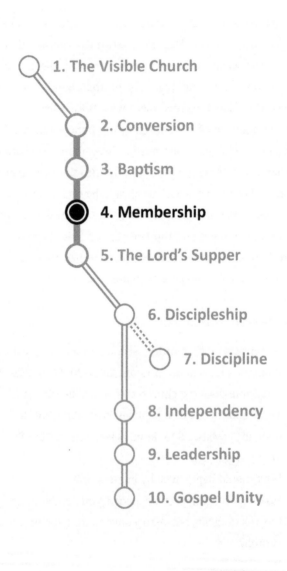

1. The Visible Church

2. Conversion

3. Baptism

4. Membership

5. The Lord's Supper

6. Discipleship

7. Discipline

8. Independency

9. Leadership

10. Gospel Unity

4. Membership
Commitment that holds a church together

Jonathan Stobbs

4. *We believe that anyone wishing to join a local church
    should be given opportunity to understand the
    responsibilities and joys of church membership, and
    thus agree to the church's statement of faith and the
    values that govern their life together (perhaps evidenced
    by the signing of a church covenant). Admission to
    membership can then occur, after:*
    i.   *the church has affirmed the candidate's profession
         of faith, evidenced by an explanation of their
         conversion and the gospel;*
    ii. *the candidate has been baptised as a believer.*

I can still remember the first time I went to Anfield, the home
of Liverpool Football Club. My uncle took me to my first game.
We lost against Blackburn Rovers. Despite that, it was an
experience I would never forget and sealed my allegiance to
the Reds. I have been back to Anfield many times since. Every
time the atmosphere has been electric. The sense of being
part of something big, songs sung passionately together,

the excitement and anticipation, the crowd lifting the team, banter in the stands, the sense of belonging to the Liverpool family, the history so full of triumph and tragedy, shared experiences – and who could fail to be moved by thousands singing 'You'll never walk alone'? A recent slogan for LFC simply encapsulates how many feel: 'This means more'. Football is where multitudes look to satisfy that longing they feel to belong. But as powerful and emotional as this is, and many other attempts by the world to try and create belonging, it always falls short.

The longing in our souls can only be satisfied by a saving relationship with Jesus Christ, belonging to him and being made part of his family. If we are believers, we have been redeemed by the sovereign grace of God, he has reconciled us to him, and we have been rescued from the dominion of the devil and brought into the kingdom of the Son of God (Col. 1:13-14). There is nothing in the world that compares to that. Similarly, there is something glorious happening when brothers and sisters in Christ join together to worship and serve the Lord side by side in a particular place, something that transcends even the experience of Anfield. *This* means more. There is nothing in the world that compares to being part of a local church. This is God's design for his people: to be knit together in committed fellowships of believers. The church, purchased with Christ's own blood, is the means that God has designed in order to proclaim and glorify his Son and accomplish his plan in the world. The local church is the universal, invisible church made visible. Therefore, believers

have the privilege, joy and responsibility to be joined to a
faithful, local manifestation of the body of Christ.

In this chapter, firstly we will consider whether
membership is biblical. Secondly, we will examine some of the
reasons why membership is set aside by many believers and
churches today. Finally, we will consider why biblical church
membership is such a blessing for the believer and vital to the
growth, maturing and stability of gospel churches.

Is church membership in the New Testament?

The word 'church' (*ekklēsia*) is found in the New Testament
110 times and at least 90 of these refer to the local church.
These local churches were defined fellowships of believers
in a particular place. For example, Acts 11:22 refers to the
'church in Jerusalem'; 1 Corinthians 1:2 refers to the 'church of
God which is at Corinth'; 1 Thessalonians is addressed 'to the
church of the Thessalonians' (1:1).[1] Paul tells the Corinthians,
'The churches of Asia greet you. Aquila and Priscilla greet you
heartily in the Lord, with the church that is in their house'
(1 Cor. 16:19). These churches met together, worshipped
together, prayed together and shared life together, but did
people join these gatherings formally or was it just a loose
association? If we look carefully at the New Testament, we see
evidence of individual believers joined together meaningfully
in local churches.

---

1   Scripture quotations in this chapter are NKJV.

Pictures of the church in the New Testament

There are several great metaphors used to describe churches in the New Testament. Four can be said to apply specifically to local churches – the body, the family, the flock and the building. Each picture teaches us something significant about the nature of the local church. However, I am going to focus on the body and the building, as they picture the strength of the bond that should exist between Christians in a local church.

The body – 1 Corinthians 12:12

'For as the body is one and has many members, but all the members of that one body, being many, are one body, so also is Christ.' Some people do not like the term 'membership', but here we see that believers are members of the body of Christ and express that membership fully in a local manifestation of that body. The local church is described here as a body with all the corresponding parts attached together. The parts are not casually fitted, intermittent, unreliable, but secured to work together in unison so that the body can function effectively. There is a common purpose and a common life because all are united under the head of the body which is Christ and him alone. It is unthinkable that one part of the body could function effectively on its own!

This is developed in Ephesians 4:15-16: '...but, speaking the truth in love, [you] may grow up in all things into him who is the head – Christ – from whom the whole body, joined and knit together by what every joint supplies, according to the effective working by which every part does its share, causes growth of the body for the edifying of itself in love.' The Lord joins his people together in local churches so that each member as part of that body can thrive and grow to his glory.

The building – Ephesians 2:21-22

'...in whom the whole building, being fitted together, grows into a holy temple in the Lord, in whom you also are being built together for a dwelling place of God in the Spirit.' A building takes shape when materials are fixed together to make the whole. If there was no membership, no unity, no submission, no proper joining together, then the building metaphor would be irrelevant. Charles Spurgeon challenged his hearers:

> I know there are some who say, 'Well, I have given myself to the Lord, but I do not intend to give myself to any church.' Now, why not? 'Because I can be a Christian without it.' Are you quite clear about that? You can be as good a Christian by disobedience to your Lord's commands as by being obedient? There is a brick. What is it made for? To help build a house. It is of no use for that brick to tell you that it is just as good a brick while it is kicking about on the ground as it would be in the house ... So you rolling-stone Christians, I do not believe you are answering your purpose. You are living contrary to the life which Christ would have you live.[2]

If the local church is the body, the building, the pillar and ground of the truth (1 Tim. 3:15), the current manifestation of Christ's kingdom and his people, then every believer who

2 Tom Carter (ed.), *Spurgeon at His Best* (Baker, 1988), 33-34.

claims to belong to him should do what they can to belong to a local church.

Early church growth and practice

In Acts 2:40-47 we see a pattern established – believe, be baptised, be added to the church, engage in the corporate life of the church. As the gospel is proclaimed, many people are genuinely converted and consequently baptised on profession of faith. These new baptised believers are added to the existing company of the Lord's first disciples (2:41). There is clear commitment and a continuing in a defined doctrinal position (2:42). Genuine fellowship showed itself as they were united in Christ, in doctrine, a corporate body together. They shared in the breaking of bread (the Lord's Supper) and prayer (2:42). This togetherness was also demonstrated in a practical love and concern for one another (2:44-45). The Lord continued to add new believers to the church daily (2:47). Reading through Acts this pattern is repeated as those who are saved are added to the church (Acts 5:14; 16:5).

The idea that you could be saved and then decide not to belong to a local church is absent from the New Testament.

In these early churches, real, loving, practical care was exercised. In 1 Timothy 5:9, Paul mentions a list of widows, suggesting the church knew which widows they had responsibility for and who were eligible for financial support. This only makes sense in the context of knowing who was part of the church and who was not, a defined membership. If they had a list for the widows, it would seem likely that there was also a general list of members who belonged to the church.

Knowing who belonged to a local church is also seen in the practice of the early church when one believer moved from one place to another. Care was given to make sure they would be received into another local church where they settled. Therefore, letters of commendation and introduction were sent to the new church in the locality to which they had moved (Acts 18:27; Rom. 16:1; 2 Cor. 3:1-2; Col. 4:10).

Join – defined in the New Testament

The word 'join' in the New Testament has a powerful meaning that should not be missed. The Greek word *kollaō* means to glue, to cement, to join firmly. It describes a formal, close dependence or bond. The same word is used by Paul to describe being joined together in a sexual relationship (1 Cor. 6:16). The word is used again to describe the profound bond of being joined to the Lord in one spirit in salvation (1 Cor. 6:17). When looking at the word in the context of the church, it only makes sense in the context of formal membership.

In Acts 5:12-14, following the judgment of Ananias and Sapphira we are told in verse 13, 'Yet none of the rest dared join them, but the people esteemed them highly.' The unbelievers who were attending the meetings at places such as Solomon's porch had great respect for the Lord's people, but this incident made them realise the seriousness of what it meant to be a recognised member of the church. There was a marked difference between being in the congregation at an open-air meeting and being glued or joined to the church as part of the company of the redeemed in that place.

Saul wanted to join the church at Jerusalem but there was a problem. 'And when Saul had come to Jerusalem, he *tried to join the disciples*; but they were all afraid of him, and did not believe that he was a disciple. But Barnabas took him and brought him to the apostles. And he declared to them how he had seen the Lord on the road, and that He had spoken to him, and how he had preached boldly at Damascus in the name of Jesus. So he was with them at Jerusalem, coming in and going out' (Acts 9:26-28). What did Saul desire to join? He would have been able to attend the public preaching. The local churches in the New Testament were bold in their desire to bring the gospel to unbelievers. The church at Jerusalem was fearful of allowing Saul to join 'the disciples', the membership, the defined body of believers in that place. They had grave doubts because of his previous reputation. It was only as Barnabas spoke on Saul's behalf before the leaders of the church that he was allowed to join them.

Church discipline

Principles for church discipline are given by the Lord Jesus Christ in Matthew 18. (This is considered in more detail in chapter 10.) The final steps of the process involve telling the church, but, unless you know who is in the church, how do you tell the church? It is impossible to get the universal church together. Without a defined body of believers in recognised membership, how do you determine who has the right to speak and vote on such a serious action? As Peter Masters summarises, 'The Saviour here puts into the hands of local churches a responsibility which proves beyond doubt that such churches should be stable, properly defined, constituted, orderly communities, not shapeless forms, with no specific membership.'[3]

Insiders and outsiders

This principle is also seen in 1 Corinthians 5 as the church at Corinth faced an issue of sexual immorality. They needed to put this man away from among them (v. 2). In verses 4-5, Paul explains how a special meeting of believers (*'when you are gathered together'*) had the authority to exclude someone guilty of serious sin from their company and all associated privileges. Such a meeting was not open to anyone, like other meetings at Corinth (1 Cor. 14:24-25) where unbelievers could attend. It was specifically a meeting of identified Christians joined together in that place to guard the purity of their gathering and to lovingly discipline the one who had fallen.

Discussing this, Paul states in strong terms the existence of insiders and outsiders: 'For what have I to do with judging those also who are outside? Do you not judge those who are inside? But those who are outside God judges' (1 Cor. 5:12-13). Insiders or outsiders of what? As we have said, unbelievers could attend the public meetings. This language can only refer to a defined body of believers in membership. The church

---

3 Peter Masters, *Church Membership in the Bible* (The Wakeman Trust, 2008), 10.

knew who was inside and who was outside. Only this type of gathering had the authority of the Lord to pass judgment on another believer in their company.

In New Testament church life, it is evident that there was a defined body of people that you could be received into or put out of. This was a people that had joined together joyfully, and willingly committed themselves under godly leadership to worship, work and witness to the glory of God.

This type of meaningful fellowship has been treasured by Christians through the generations and has been a specific distinctive of reformed Baptist churches.[4] They saw that this was not only for the benefit of individual believers in their ongoing walk with the Lord, but also in obedience to his commands. Which leads to the question, why are so many believers and churches averse to church membership?

---

4 The 1689 Baptist Confession of Faith highlights this in section 26, clause 5, explaining that it is the clear command of the head of the church, Jesus Christ, that local churches should be established to fulfil his purposes on the earth to the glory of his name. Clause 6 goes on to describe the nature of those local churches: 'The members of these churches are saints by calling, visibly displaying and demonstrating in and by their profession and life their obedience to the call of Christ. They willingly agree to live together according to Christ's instructions, giving themselves to the Lord and to one another by the will of God, with the stated purpose of following the ordinances of the gospel' (Rom. 1:7; 1 Cor. 1:2; Acts 2:41-42; Acts 5:13-14; 2 Cor. 9:15). The framers of the confession saw a biblical order through a living relationship with Christ, in public profession, baptism, membership and a commitment to the corporate life of a local church.

Taking a pass on membership

During the years that I have served as a pastor, I can think of many conversations on this issue I have had at various times with believers who have been at the church. They wanted the benefits of fellowship but without any accountability. Sometimes those conversations were difficult, sometimes confusing, but always very sad that there should be such a resistance to publicly identifying with the local church.

Sometimes it was clear that some brothers and sisters had endured damaging experiences of being part of a church elsewhere which had left deep scars and a reluctance to make themselves vulnerable again. There were some who just did not like the idea that only baptised believers should be welcomed into membership. Other conversations just highlighted a low view of the church and a strong reaction against any form of submission or commitment. These objections are no doubt magnified on a wider scale. So why is there such resistance to membership?

There are some believers who have just never really considered the issue of church membership before and its importance for the health of the believer and the local church. If that is your position, I would encourage you to keep searching the Scriptures on this.

Apart from that, many other possible reasons could be explored, but I would suggest that one of the major factors is that we live in a culture that is generally fearful of commitment. Our society has been influenced by what Robert

Bellah has called 'expressive individualism'.[5] This attitude sees the individual committed to personal flourishing with the focus on getting their specific needs and desires met. Consequently, the individual has the ultimate authority on what they believe is truth and how they define their identity. This has meant that there has been a shift away from any external expectation or authority, specifically in the realm of faith. So an individual no longer needs the church for teaching, authority or accountability but only to serve their desires for a subjective, spiritual experience. To a greater or lesser extent many are touched by this way of thinking and so are reluctant to commit to one place. They want the flexibility to move around depending on what meets their needs at any particular time. No church is perfect and no church can meet every personalised desire. If churches only focus on trying to please people it does not take much to drift from solid biblical moorings and for gospel focus to be lost.

Expressive individualism may not have entirely gripped many believers but touches of its influence are felt. The problem is that true biblical Christianity means the individual lays down their own will to the Lordship of Christ. We are either in Christ on his terms or we are not. The gospel is not a consumer product. The call of Christ is to deny self, take up the cross and follow him. As Brett McCracken writes:

5 See Robert Bellah, Richard Madsen, William Sullivan, Ann Swidler and Steven Tipton, *Habits of the Heart: Individualism and Commitment in American Life* (University of California Press, 1985).

Christian discipleship is not consumer-friendly. Further, Jesus calls us not to individualised, self-styled spirituality but to faith in community, accountable to others. Christianity dis-embedded from the church is not really Christianity. It feigns to embrace Jesus while shunning his body (see 1 Cor. 12; Eph. 1:22-23; 5:23; Col. 1:18) ... When a church becomes less about the demands of Scripture and more about the demands of individuals on the church to fit their preferences, it loses its power to transform us and subvert our idols. It becomes a commodity to be shopped for, consumed and then abandoned when another, shinier, trendier, more 'relevant' option appears.[6]

Generally, we are living in a non-committal age where neither non-Christians nor even many believers have any strong inclination to give themselves to something or to others for the long term. Therefore the idea of joining a church is not easily embraced. However, regardless of prevailing trends in society, membership of a local church for a believer is the desire and command of Christ. Many have said it – one of the most counter-cultural things a believer can do is to become an engaged member of a faithful local church.

What is required for church membership?

If a believer wants to join a church, what is needed? It is not about making people jump through hoops, or trying to be exclusive, although membership is exclusive in so far

---

6   Brett McCracken, 'Church Shopping with Charles Taylor', in Collin Hansen (ed.), *Our Secular Age* (The Gospel Coalition, 2017), 80-81.

as there is a desire to protect the local church family from wolves and bring genuine sheep into the pen. Following the recommendation of the leaders, it is the church which decides who is to be welcomed and affirmed. What are the requirements?

A real profession of faith – unless a person has been genuinely converted and has a saving relationship with Jesus Christ they cannot be a member of a local church. To help in this, churches often have a statement of faith to ensure that there is a clarity in what the church believes from the Bible and what the person believes. This is to affirm believers in the truth. The real profession magnifies not what the individual has done, but what Christ has done and the wonders of his saving grace.

Baptism as a believer – baptism does not save. Rather, it publicly identifies the believer with Christ and is also the local church publicly identifying someone as a true Christian.[7]

The blessing of belonging

Life in a local church is a great thing, but it can be difficult at times. It will never be perfect because the church is full of imperfect believers. But, no matter how weak things may appear, the local church is precious to the Lord Jesus Christ. If we love him we will love what he loves. 'Christ also loved the church and gave himself for her' (Eph. 5:25). It was Christ's

---

7 For an excellent in-depth treatment of why baptism is required for church membership please see Bobby Jamieson, *Going Public* (B&H Academic, 2015).

love for the church that saw him give himself for her. Those who love the Lord Jesus Christ will demonstrate the attitude of Christ in loving the church. Being joined together with brothers and sisters in Christ in that defined local family, an outpost of the kingdom, is a high responsibility and stunning privilege. Dr. Martyn Lloyd Jones said, 'We must grasp once again the idea of church membership as being the membership of the body of Christ and as the biggest honour which can come a man's way in this world.'[8] Why is it a blessing to belong in this way?

By belonging to a local church, the believer is affirmed as a citizen of Christ's kingdom. To be received into the membership of a Bible-believing, rightly led, loving fellowship is a great means of assurance. It is a mutual affirmation that the believer's faith is genuine, their profession credible and their lifestyle and conduct showing signs of new life in Christ. They are identified as part of the body in that place.

By belonging to a local church, the believer stands openly with Christ and his people in the world. Joining a local body of believers is a clear declaration to everyone that you are not ashamed of Christ or his people. You are one of the 'living stones' being built together for a dwelling place of God in the Spirit.

By belonging to a local church, the believer is kept from an unhelpful isolated independence. Without the fellowship of believers to sharpen, soften, challenge love, it is easy

---

8   D. Martyn Lloyd Jones, Knowing the Times (The Banner of Truth Trust, 1989), 30.

for believers to develop an unbalanced position which is detrimental to their spiritual wellbeing. Believers also need the regular, God-ordained, balanced teaching ministry of a local church to mature and grow in godliness.

By belonging to a local church, the believer enables godly leaders to fulfil their calling effectively and encourages the ongoing ministry of that church. Hebrews 13:17 says, 'Obey those who rule over you, and be submissive, for they watch out for your souls, as those who must give account. Let them do so with joy and not with grief, for that would be unprofitable for you.' As a pastor, before the Lord, I take my responsibility to care for the Christians placed into my charge incredibly seriously (1 Pet. 5:3). But how could I be a faithful under-shepherd if I did not know who is in that flock and who is not? Elders can only shepherd the people and give an account to God if they know who they are. The elders of a church are not responsible for the spiritual wellbeing of every individual who visits the church or who attends occasionally. They are primarily responsible to shepherd those who have submitted to the care and authority of the elders through membership of the local church.

Belonging to a local church strengthens the impact of a believer's gospel witness. A believer who has a spiritual home, part of a united loving community, is in a better place to put Christ on display and proclaim his name in this fractured and broken world.

Belonging to a local church gives us a place to develop everyone's gifts. God in his kindness has given all Christians spiritual gifts. This is not for the benefit of the individual alone or any self-promotion but for the building up of the body. These spiritual gifts are given to us, not for self-serving reasons, but to learn how to submit ourselves and our resources for the good of his people (1 Cor. 12:7; 14:12, 26). As a believer loves and serves the church body willingly, their gifts will become evident. The local church provides a loving and encouraging environment where members can discover their gifts and be given opportunities to use them for God's glory and the benefit of his church.

Life in the family

Being a member of a local body of Christ sees the believer placed within a spiritual family in which they can thrive and grow. Our Christian lives are meant to involve meaningful care and concern for others. When the believer is a recognised part of the body, they are able to receive genuine care from others in the body who are committed to their spiritual good. It also allows the believer to display the love of Christ in similar affection and action to others in that particular household of faith.

Sometimes churches use a membership covenant to define a local body's commitment to trust Christ, worship God and love each other in ways commanded in the New Testament. Members agree to the church covenant in which their responsibilities towards God and their fellow believers are outlined. Following my conversion and baptism as a young person, I was received into membership at a Grace Baptist church in the north-west of England. Part of their practice was to use a church covenant.[9] Once a year the members would affirm their commitment before the Lord to those covenant responsibilities to live to his glory and to honour Christ in serving him as a fellowship.

Church covenant or not, biblical membership must be meaningful. It must demonstrate the outworking of John 13:34-35: 'A new commandment I give to you, that you love one another; as I have loved you, that you also love one another. By this all will know that you are My disciples, if you have love for one another.' What does that look like? Bobby Jamieson explains:

> It means you are radically, inextricably attached to the body. It means you don't primarily define yourself as an individual but as part of a whole. Practically, church members should attend church consistently. They should pray with and for the church. They should give. They should serve. They should bear one another's burdens. They should knit their lives to one another so tightly that if you try to pull one member out of the body, another dozen come with him, pulling him back in.[10]

This togetherness comes as members take their responsibilities seriously and joyfully. Being part of a local church is the best avenue for serving the Lord. Let me give you some ways church members can do this:

---

9   See Appendix for Grace Baptist Church Southport's covenant.

10   Jamieson, *Going Public*, 219.

- *Attend regularly* – 'And let us consider one another in order to stir up love and good works, not forsaking the assembling of ourselves together, as is the manner of some, but exhorting one another, and so much the more as you see the Day approaching' (Heb. 10:24-25). A church member honours the Lord, will be blessed and will be a blessing to their brothers and sisters if they make being at all the church gatherings a priority. This also includes meetings concerning the business of the church.

- *Pray for the church* – One of the simplest ways the church members can edify and encourage their brothers and sisters towards greater obedience, holiness and joy in Christ is through prayer. As they pray for the cause of Christ and his people in that church their hearts will be warmed. The church will not flourish without the prayers of her members.

- *Give generously* – A church member should be a wise steward of the resources that the Lord has given to them. The wellbeing of the church, the ongoing ministry and gospel witness at home and abroad should be heart-felt concerns and supporting them generously is pleasing to the Lord.

- *Get involved* – The responsibility of every member in the church is to be about the Master's work in the big things and little things. It may be visiting the sick, visiting other members, giving hospitality, helping with the youth work, being involved in outreach, coming alongside those young in the faith, writing letters, to name but a few. There is always a way to be useful to the Lord and his people.

- *Live out the 'one anothers'* – Every member should see the emphasis the New Testament places on those in a local church engaging in a deep way with one another. There are just under sixty 'one another' exhortations in the New Testament. Think about the following: love one another (John 13:35); serve one another (Gal. 5:13); forgive one another (Eph. 4:32); encourage one another (1 Thess. 5:11); instruct one another (Rom. 15:14); comfort one another (1 Thess. 4:18); carry one another's burdens (Gal. 6:2); admonish one another (Col. 3:16). These and the many other 'one anothers' direct Christians in the ways they should be sharing their lives with other Christians. Salvation is God's work. The church is to recognise and affirm individuals in whom that miraculous saving work is taking place. The church is also the context for their discipleship, the setting in which disciples help each other as members of the body to grow in Christ, serve together and reach out with the gospel that others may become disciples too. What can be seen here through the 'one anothers' is that being a member of a church is never passive, but rather, it is a willing, loving, fulfilling life lived together with brothers and sisters in Christ.

When these things are present in the life of the church it will be a loving community that shows the love of Christ working in and through them. Andrew King explores further in chapter 6 what this shared life of discipleship looks like in a local church. Sometimes that discipleship may mean the need to admonish, rebuke and, sadly, discipline a member of the church who has gone astray. Though this is painful, the local church is the setting for true loving discipline to be administered. Nigel Graham explains that in chapter 7.

Conclusion

Biblical church membership draws the line between the church and the world. It identifies a people saved by grace, bound together by their fellowship in the Lord Jesus Christ. It really is a wonderful privilege and a gift of grace to belong to the family of God and a local manifestation of that family. To join a particular church shows your love for Christ and for his people. Life together in a church is not always easy and is sometimes painful and that is because there is still a sanctifying work being done in our lives as believers. But that is why belonging to a local church with faithful ministry and meaningful membership is vital. As Paul says in Ephesians 4:12-13 these things are given '...for the equipping of the saints for the work of ministry, for the edifying of the body of Christ, till we all come to the unity of the faith and of the knowledge of the Son of God, to a perfect man, to the measure of the stature of the fullness of Christ.'

The nature of a local church is counter-cultural, other-worldly, but it is Christ's design and the means through which we are to impact the world to exalt and proclaim his glorious name. There really is nothing like it in all the world.

Questions for discussion

1. Why do some believers and churches downplay the importance of church membership?

2. Where in the Bible would you go to show that church membership is biblical?

3. What blessings from biblical church membership have you experienced?

4. Would you say your own church membership is meaningful at this moment? What steps can you take to connect and grow?

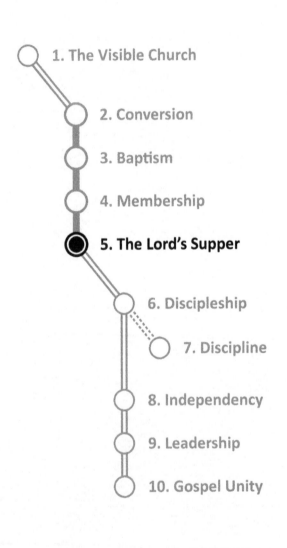

1. The Visible Church

2. Conversion

3. Baptism

4. Membership

5. The Lord's Supper

6. Discipleship

7. Discipline

8. Independency

9. Leadership

10. Gospel Unity

5. The Lord's Supper

The clearest expression of communion

Matthew Benton

5. *We believe that the Lord's Supper is:*

   i. *a local church's act of communing with Christ and each other, and of commemorating Christ's death by partaking of bread and wine;*

   ii. *a converted, baptised person's act of receiving Christ's benefits and renewing his or her commitment to Christ and his people;*

   iii. *Christ's ongoing means of binding the members of a local church together as one body and marking it off from the world;*

   iv. *for baptised members of local churches, whether members of the church where the Supper is being celebrated, or visitors in good standing at another gospel church.*

It has long been suggested that the health of family life is strengthened by eating together. It is not, of course, that simply eating together makes you family – that happens by other means – but the family meal table is glue for family life.

Imagine a household in which blood-related people lived, and yet they never ate together. Could you call that collection of people a family?

It is not simply that all human beings have to eat and drink. While growing up, my brothers and I may have resembled pigs at a trough sometimes, yet something else happened round that family table over the months and years. Laughter and tears, songs and stories, memories created, relationships deepened, the family strengthened. Meals greatly enhance community. One writer suggests that nothing unites man and man more than eating and drinking together.[1]

Just as eating together is important for the health of family life, so with God and his people. This chapter seeks to argue that participating in the Lord's Supper is not to be understood in purely personal terms, as some type of sacramental grace from God to the individual. Rather, in the language of Oliver O'Donovan, it is about the 'formation of the body'.[2] From the outside looking in, it is the ongoing means by which the church is defined and made visible, in a particular place, in a particular moment in time. Inside the church, through participation in this meal, God's people are reminded of the means, but also the reality, of their being God's people. It is a meal through which God's people are marked out

---

1   Bertold Klappert, 'Lord's Supper', in C. Brown (ed.), New International Dictionary of New Testament Theology, Vol 2, (Zondervan, 2008), 520.

2   Oliver O'Donovan, Desire of the Nations (Cambridge University Press, 1996), 180.

and bound together and as such should be at the centre of church life.

This chapter will examine a biblical understanding of the Lord's Supper from these two angles. Firstly, from the outside looking in, we will seek to capture a sense of what is happening as a local church gathers to celebrate the Lord's Supper. Then secondly, from the inside, partaking of the Lord's Supper, we will ask who the Supper is for and in what sense individually we partake.

From the outside looking in: the church made visible in space and time

My desire here is to help us understand from the Scriptures what we observe as the church gathers to celebrate the Lord's Supper. However, before I go further, let me explain an assumption that I have made. Our statement[3] says that the Lord's Supper is an act of the local church. I believe that will be self-explanatory by the end of this chapter. Indeed, the New Testament gives no solid evidence of a local church celebrating the Lord's Supper other than all together. The very clear emphasis of 1 Corinthians 11 is that of the church in Corinth coming together as a whole church, as one family, as those who should be concerned for the wellbeing of one another, waiting for one another, participating together as those who share together in the body and blood of Christ

---

3   We are indebted to Bobby Jamieson for the wording in this clause of our statement. See Jamieson, *Going Public* (B&H Academic, 2015).

(1 Cor. 11:18, 20, 33-34; 1 Cor. 10:16). Justin Martyr, writing in the second century, indicates that the regular practice of the early church was to celebrate the Supper at the 'common assembly' where 'all the believers who lived in a town' gathered.[4] The Lord's Supper is celebrated by the local church gathered as a body, feasting in the presence of the Lord.

This imagery of feasting together in the presence of the Lord is one that the Old Testament returns to again and again to describe the blessing and friendship of God. Abraham prepared a feast for the Lord in Genesis 18. Most memorably in Psalm 23 we read, 'You prepare a table before me in the presence of my enemies.'[5] Or again, the end time imagery in Isaiah 25 speaks of the Lord preparing a lavish banquet of aged wine, with the best cuts of meat for all peoples. The life and blessing of the kingdom is portrayed in the language of food and drink.[6] So when Jesus announces in Luke 7, 'The Son of Man came eating and drinking', he is saying more than simply that Jesus is fun to be around. Rather, with him comes abundant life and blessing, the joy and fellowship of God.[7]

---

4   Quoted in Nick Needham, 2000 *Years of Christ's Power*, Vol 1 (Christian Focus/Grace Publications, 2016), 72-73.

5   Scripture quotations in this chapter are from the NIV.

6   See also Genesis 9:17-21; 18:1-15.

7   See also John 2:1-11, Jesus' first miracle announces something similar at the wedding in Cana.

Jesus is King

Above all, the gift of food in the Bible is understood as a royal gift, the work of the King. In John 6, after the feeding of the five thousand, Jesus withdrew from the crowds because he knew that the crowd 'intended to come and make him king by force' (6:15). The miracle was not lost on those Jewish diners. The Old Testament recounts and pictures kings and rulers as beneficent providers. A king was the 'host with the most'.[8] Think about Melchizedek, the king of righteousness and peace, offering food and drink to Abram, or Joseph feeding the nations as ruler under Pharaoh. Then perhaps most remarkably in 2 Samuel 9, where David, in an act of incredible mercy, restores to Saul's grandson, Mephibosheth, all of the family's land and gives him a seat at the king's table.[9] Yet these are but echoes of the greater benevolence of the Lord God who feeds his people Israel with bread from heaven and water from the rock.

Jesus in his feeding miracles was demonstrating that he is the King feeding his people. Even those tax collectors and sinners considered beyond the reach of restoration are welcomed to his table (Luke 15:1-2). Then on the night he was to be betrayed, Jesus institutes and hosts another meal. As we read the accounts of the Last Supper, we see the same imagery – Jesus the King gathering people round a table, providing for their every need and calling them friends.

---

8   See 2 Samuel 6:19; 1 Kings 3:15; Esther 1:3.

9   See Genesis 14:18; 41:57; 2 Samuel 9.

Jesus and the Passover

The context for this meal is, of course, the Passover. Not only does Jesus gather with his disciples that evening to eat the Passover, but in Jesus' very words, by which he initiates his Supper, he links it with the Passover:

> 'I have eagerly desired to eat this Passover with you before I suffer. For I tell you, I will not eat it again until it finds fulfilment in the kingdom of God.' After taking the cup, he gave thanks and said, 'Take this and divide it among you. For I tell you I will not drink again from the fruit of the vine until the kingdom of God comes.' And he took bread, gave thanks and broke it, and gave it to them, saying, 'This is my body given for you; do this in remembrance of me'. (Luke 22:15-19)

On the night before God brought his people out of Egypt, he told them to prepare a meal. It is almost impossible to overstate the significance of this meal. It marked out the people whom God would save. The blood on the door frames meant life. It was the sign for them that the angel of death would pass over their houses.

God told his people to celebrate this meal every year as a memorial, as a reminder of God's saving work. This meal marked the birth of a nation, the defining moment in their history.[10] Foreigners could not celebrate the Passover. If

---

10   Indeed the feasts of Israel define them as a people. The Passover recalled the rescue from Egypt. The feast of Tabernacles recalled their time in the wilderness. The feast of Pentecost linked to God's provision of the harvest. The feast of Purim recalled God's deliverance in the time of Esther. The feast of Jubilee looked

they wanted to, then males of their household needed to be circumcised. They would need to identify as members of the Lord's people (Exod. 12:48-49). It was a meal that the whole nation was commanded to celebrate. As generation after generation ate this meal, fathers were to tell their sons, 'I do this because of what the Lord did for me when I came out of Egypt' (Exod. 13:8). Each Passover was to be a present-day reminder of what God had done for all those gathered around the table, by means of God's covenant with his people.

Commemorating and communing

When Jesus says that he eagerly desires to 'eat this Passover' with his disciples, he is instituting a new meal of liberation. It is a meal to be celebrated in order to remember our salvation through the blood work of Jesus on the cross. It is a meal that celebrates a new covenant. As Jesus takes the bread and later the cup he calls his disciples to 'do this in remembrance of me' (Luke 22:19; 1 Cor. 11:24-25). The meal itself pictures afresh for us the sacrificial work of Christ on our behalf, as the bread is broken and the wine is poured out.

Like the celebration of the Passover, the Lord's Supper is more than simply remembering a historical event; it is a meal of covenantal remembrance, bringing the past into the present.[11] We respond to Jesus' words, 'This is my body, which is for you; do this in remembrance of me .... This cup is the

forward to God's final redemption of his people.

11 Bobby Jamieson, *Understanding the Lord's Supper* (B&H Academic, 2018), 27-28.

new covenant in my blood; do this, whenever you drink it, in remembrance of me', by partaking of bread and wine. In doing so we identify again with Christ's saving work. Together, as a local church, we announce our belonging to Christ and so in that place, in that moment in time, we make visible God's people, the church in that place.

In this act the gathered local church is at the same time 'communing with Christ and each other' as our statement says. In John's account of the Last Supper, he makes clear that Jesus is the King who de-robes to wash his disciples' feet. He is the one who as the King gathers his disciples round the table, breaks bread with them and calls them 'friends'.[12] So the Supper is a reflection not only on the suffering of Christ but also on his achievements at the cross. As we proclaim the Lord's death, through this meal, we proclaim his victory over sin, death and hell.[13] As we look on at the local church gathered together around the Lord's Table, partaking of his Supper, we observe those feasting together in the presence of the Lord. The cross, having made this people clean, enables them to gather as friends around the King's table to feast with him. In doing so, there is made visible in the present the

---

12   Although John's account of the Last Supper does not include the words of institution, his words clearly recall Jesus as God's King (John 13:1-17). He is the King who gathers his friends and calls them to love each other in the light of his love and live under his rule (John 15:9-17), and to do so through understanding their identity as God's people, in Christ (John 15:1-8). These are all things we affirm through our participation in the Supper.

13   Peter Leithart, *The Kingdom and the Power* (P&R, 2012), 121-122.

anticipation of the day when we will feast with Christ face to face. Jesus himself anticipated this at the Last Supper when he said, 'I tell you, I will not drink from this fruit of the vine from now on until that day when I drink it new *with you* in my Father's kingdom' (Matt. 26:29).[14]

In other words, this meal is a foretaste of the full breaking in of God's kingdom which is yet to come. Peter Leithart evokes this wonderfully:

> At the Lord's Table we receive an initial taste of the final heavens and earth, but the Lord's Supper is not merely a sign of the eschatological feast, as if there were two separate feasts. Instead the Supper is the early stages of that very feast. Every time we celebrate the Lord's Supper we are displaying in history a glimpse of the end of history and anticipating in this world the order of the world that is to come.[15]

Consequently, this meal is very much 'a local church's act,' precisely because the local church is, as this book has argued for, and as Jonathan Leeman puts it, 'where and how a Christian formally assumes citizenship in Christ's kingdom, thereby making Christ's presence on earth public in a particular place and time.'[16] The church gathered celebrating the Lord's Supper should make visible the Lord's people in that place and time. This means the Lord's Supper should not just be considered an ordinance of the universal church.

---

14   Emphasis added. See also Luke 22:18.

15   Peter Leithart, *Blessed are the Hungry* (Canon Press, 2000), 14-15.

16   Jonathan Leeman, *Political Church* (IVP Academic, 2016), 362.

To consider it in such terms takes away the significance of what is being proclaimed (1 Cor. 11:26). Proclaiming the Lord's death until he comes is to make visible the breaking in of the kingdom that comes through his death, in a particular town in a particular moment in history. Here is the local church, a picture in time and space of the church universal. Therefore to participate, on a regular basis, is to declare oneself part of the body, the church, and therefore it is for church members. As our statement says, it is, 'Christ's ongoing means of binding the members of a local church together as one body and marking it off from the world.'

From the inside partaking of: the many becoming one in Christ

We have seen that as we look on at the celebration of the Lord's Supper, we view a communal meal instituted by Jesus that defines a people as those bought by Christ, belonging to him. It is the ongoing means by which the church is defined and made visible, in a particular place, in a particular moment in time.

So what is it like to be on the inside, as an individual participating in this meal? The most common answer would be to talk simply in terms of remembrance. Jesus commanded his disciples to 'do this in remembrance of me' (1 Cor. 11:24, 25). But it seems that the Bible sees the Supper as more than just an *aide-memoire*.

Firstly, to partake is also to acknowledge the authority of this King. Again, the contours of the Old Testament help us understand this. The gift of food from the King also acknowledges that one is subject to that King. Whom you are willing to sup with seems to have great implications in the Bible; it is not a casual thing, but a covenant-ratifying act.

The opening chapter of Daniel recounts how Daniel and his friends, having been brought into the royal court of Babylon, are 'assigned' a daily portion of the food and wine that the king ate and drank. Daniel and his friends see partaking of the royal food and wine as an act of defilement (Dan. 1:8). Many argue that what was on the menu would have caused the defilement. However, the passage itself speaks more about whose food it was, rather than what food it was. Daniel and his friends have been exiled, made subjects of a new king, but Daniel underlines by refusing the gift of the king's food that Nebuchadnezzar is not ultimately his king. For Daniel and his friends, as the rest of the book underlines, they serve the eternal King who provides for their every need.

Contrast that dietary decision with that of the first man and woman in the garden. Told by God that they may eat of any of the trees of the garden apart from the tree of the knowledge of good and evil, they make their own menu choice. That infamous meal takes place not under the authority of God, but under the serpent's deception. It is a meal of rebellious defiance that breaks fellowship with God, declaring independence from the rule of God the creator. In a similar fashion, in Exodus 32, another meal is recorded as Aaron and the people worship the golden calf. It is an act that identifies them and unites them in their idolatry (Exod. 32:6).[17] It seems there is a covenantal significance to the eating of such meals that identifies them to be in willing submission to the rule of the benefactor of the food. There is, then, a sense that whose table you eat at announces who you are.

Marking off and binding

In 1 Corinthians 10, Paul references that episode in Exodus 32 as he speaks of the dangers of idolatry. It may seem to some that he makes a huge leap in his argument, as by 10:16 he brings us to the Lord's Table. Yet if, as we have seen, under whose jurisdiction we eat matters because it reflects loyalty and willing submission, then to eat at the Table of the Lord must communicate that we are willing to submit to the rule of Christ.

Paul puts it bluntly in 10:21: 'You cannot drink the cup of the Lord and the cup of demons too; you cannot have a part in both the Lord's Table and the table of demons.' Paul is making a crucial point about a person's participation in the Lord's Table. Again the table that we eat at defines us as one people. 'Is not the cup of thanksgiving for which we give thanks a participation in the blood of Christ? Because there is one loaf, we, who are many, are one body, for we all share the one loaf' (1 Cor. 10:16-17). To participate is to share with others in the

---

17   Interestingly when Moses approached the camp, he took the calf, burnt it, ground it down, scattered it on the water and 'made the Israelites drink it', uniting the idolaters ever more tightly to their idol (Exod. 32:20).

blood of Christ. To eat of the one loaf is to announce that we are united as one body. The contrast is made in verse 19 and 20: while false gods are nothing, by getting involved with them you are associating with what is ultimately not from God and therefore demonic.

Receiving and renewing

Participating in the Lord's Supper declares us to be God's people living under his rule. This hugely raises the bar of our understanding of the Lord's Supper because we are each declaring to which side we belong.

As our statement says, to partake is to receive Christ's benefits. To take of the bread and the cup is then to feed spiritually upon Christ. As Calvin puts it, the Lord's Supper is the means by which Christ 'transfuses his life into us'.[18] Partaking in the Supper is to be given a present seal of God's promises to us in Christ, thereby strengthening our faith in his work. The Lord's Supper leads me to rediscover again that my worth and righteousness are found in Jesus' blood and righteousness alone. I am forgiven, united with Christ, and made a member of God's household, the church. The Lord's Supper works alongside the gospel word not only to remind but also to make the gospel a felt reality, as through our taking of the physical elements the Spirit makes known his presence with us.[19]

---

18   John Calvin, Institutes, 4.17.10.

19   This is helpfully explained in Carl Trueman, Grace Alone (Zondervan, 2017), 212-214.

Such fellowship with Christ by means of the Lord's Supper tangibly reaffirms that I am not only joined to Christ but also I am joined to those with whom I eat. As we share together in the blood and body of Christ we are reminded that, for each of us, our worth and righteousness is in our Saviour. We all share of the same loaf and so 'we who are many are one body' (1 Cor. 10:17).

In 1 Corinthians 11, as Paul gives instructions in regard to the Lord's Supper, he emphasises the togetherness it expresses. He reiterates the same word, 'together' (*synerchomai*) five times in verses 17, 18, 20, 33 and 34. This togetherness reminds us that being united to Christ means that we are united to one another. We are one body and so the Lord's Supper is the reminder that we are family. The Supper is the glue for the life of the local church.

When God made a covenant with Israel at Sinai, we are told in Exodus 24 that that covenant was signed off not just by the blood of the sacrifice but by a covenant meal hosted by God. In 1 Corinthians 11:25 we are told that the Lord's Supper is a sign of the new covenant, a covenant inaugurated by the once-and-for-all sacrifice of Jesus but ratified again and again in a meal that Jesus hosts. Yet as we renew our commitment to Christ, at the same time we are renewing our commitment to his people. We are recognising again that we are one body. Again in 1 Corinthians 11 we see this very specific connection between the proclamation of the Lord's death around the Table and demonstrating loving care towards one's brothers and sisters.

> For whenever you eat this bread and drink this cup, you proclaim the Lord's death until he comes. So then, whoever eats the bread or drinks the cup of the Lord in an unworthy manner will be guilty of sinning against the body and blood of the Lord. Everyone ought to examine themselves before they eat of the bread and drink from the cup. For those who eat and drink without discerning the body of Christ eat and drink judgment on themselves. (1 Cor. 11:26-29)

Notice that judgment is brought by a person upon themselves not because they do not discern in enough depth the mysteries of the Godhead. Rather it is through eating and drinking without discerning the 'body of Christ' that they eat and drink judgment on themselves. In the context of the passage, in which Paul is challenging the behaviour of some in the church towards their fellow brothers and sisters when it comes to the Lord's Supper, it seems best to understand the phrase 'the body of Christ' as the local church. It suggests that those who eat of the Lord's Supper and say, 'it really doesn't matter who else is here today because this is just about me and Jesus', or as was happening in Corinth, 'we are not going to wait for them,' are people who 'drink judgment upon themselves'. They do so because this meal is about the rule of the kingdom made manifest, in which we demonstrate not only love for God but also love for one another.

Paul is saying that as we participate in the Lord's Supper we don't simply look back to the death of Christ, upward to his rule now and forward to the day of his return, but we look around to see again his blood-bought people to whom we are joined as family. We rejoice in the reality of the breaking in of the kingdom and therefore the fellowship into which he has brought us.

Who should be at the Table?

Given that partaking in the Lord's Supper is to renew one's commitment to Christ and his people, the Table must, of course, only be open firstly to those who have turned from their sin and turned to Christ in repentance and faith. At the same time, because the Lord's Supper is an act of the local church, that repentance and faith must be publicly recognised through baptism and church membership, as previous chapters have sought to express.

When Paul places so much emphasis on this act as being an expression of our unity as God's people, and our re-commitment to Christ and his people, participation at the Table must be linked with public commitment to the people through church membership. The fact that disregard of some others in the Corinthian congregation led to judgment demonstrates the seriousness of the Lord's Supper as a covenant-ratifying act.

For many, such a stance seems harsh and ungenerous: why are you advocating preventing access to this means of grace for those who claim to trust in Christ? Yet, as I have sought to demonstrate, the Supper is not a private devotion but a communal meal in which we not only receive but reaffirm that we are Christ's body by his grace (1 Cor. 10:16-17). To participate regularly without real commitment to a local church shows a disregard for Christ's people which Paul warns against. There is an awesome seriousness to proclaiming something that is not true in the practice of our lives. 1 Corinthians 11 underlines the seriousness of being uninterested in meaningful fellowship with real brothers and sisters in Christ. It is like turning up at a family dinner and then not only leaving before the clearing up is done, but also not showing any real interest in the family before, during or after the meal.

Equally if this is a church act, the church must be able to assess whether someone is in a position to take the Lord's Supper. 1 Corinthians 10:21 underscores the danger of sharing in the benefits of Christ's work while misunderstanding the gospel. The church is to avoid the danger of giving false assurance of a person's salvation. A non-believer participating in the Lord's Supper gives false assurance. This has always been the concern of the church. Writing in the second century, Justin Martyr speaks of the Eucharist, 'which no-one is allowed to share unless he believes that the things we teach are true, and has been washed with the washing that is for the forgiveness of sins and the second birth, and is living as Christ commanded'.[20] Or as the Didache puts it clearly, 'let none eat or drink of your Eucharist, but such that have been baptised into the name of the Lord.'[21] In the New Testament

---

20 Quoted in Needham, 2000 Years of Christ's Power, Vol 1, 73.

21 Didache 9:5 translated by Charles H. Hoole, http://www. earlychristianwritings.com/text/didache-hoole.html [accessed 12/06/18].

the ordinance of baptism is the means by which repentance and faith are publicly expressed and affirmed (Acts 2:38).

Our statement says that the Lord's Supper is for 'baptised members of local churches, whether members of the church where the Supper is being celebrated, or visitors in good standing at another gospel church.' This is intended not in an exclusive but in a loving way. How this is managed within a local church may look different in different situations. Some churches have a separate service for those who are church members and for visiting believers who are willing to have their testimony of faith in Christ affirmed by an elder of the church. Others will verbally set out clearly God's requirements for participation at the Table.

Either way the local church is recognising that both the ordinances of baptism and the Lord's Supper exist to give ongoing definition to the local church as the outpost of the kingdom in a particular place, at a particular time. Without the proper utilisation of these ordinances the church relies simply on the self-identification of conversion by the recipient of the Supper, and has no loving mechanism by which that person can be informed of false assurance. One acknowledges that the church's use of the keys of the kingdom (Matt. 16:19; 18:15-20) working through the ordinances has the potential to be as fallible as the human beings who make up the church. Yet precisely because it is the assembly that is given the keys by Christ, that means that there must be some checks and balances in their wielding this power.

Conclusion

Sharing meals as family is the glue of family life, not only the opportunity to eat but also the chance to grow together and care for one another. So should the Lord's Supper be in the life of the local church. It is not just an opportunity for private devotions but a chance to be family, to welcome new members, to rejoice with those who rejoice, to mourn with those who mourn, supporting one another through prayer and scriptural encouragement. At its centre, it is the meal in which we rediscover our identity together, rejoice in our liberty, renew our fidelity to our Saviour and emphasise our unity. Yet such an experience only comes when we understand and recognise one another as family. This family is given definition and strengthened through the gospel order for which this book seeks to argue.

Whenever we celebrate the Lord's Supper, as much as is humanly possible we should be visually picturing the world to come, declaring the victory of Christ's cross. We make visible the kingdom of God, God's blood-bought people, gathered around the Table of the King, feasting as family as we will do for ever.

Questions for discussion

1. What does feasting have to do with the relationship between God and his people?

2. Looking in from outside, what is happening when a local church gathers to celebrate the Lord's Supper?

3. What does it mean to be on the inside, an individual participating in this meal?

4. The Lord's Supper should be considered an ordinance for the local church and not the universal church. How does the author justify this understanding from the Bible?

5. How has this chapter grown your appreciation for the Lord's Supper in the life of the local church? Will you approach the next Supper any differently as a result?

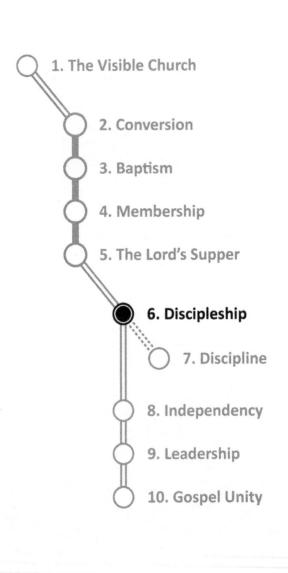

1. The Visible Church

2. Conversion

3. Baptism

4. Membership

5. The Lord's Supper

6. Discipleship

7. Discipline

8. Independency

9. Leadership

10. Gospel Unity

6. Discipleship

The formative instruction of all members

Andrew King

> 6. We believe that each local church should be characterised by a shared life of discipleship. As all the members are equipped, they should be encouraged to use their gifts to serve others in various works of ministry and prayer. Together, each local church is to grow in holiness as Christ's bride and in witness as his ambassadors to the watching world. Local church life is to be a growing display of heaven on earth.

Congratulations, you've got the job! But how will you be trained and equipped to do it?

One option would be for you to arrive on your first day at work and just 'pick it up as you go along'. It might be possible to watch others if they were doing the same thing, but what if your job has differences? And what if you were expected to use expensive machinery or fly a passenger jet? Another option might be to book on to some residential training courses or to watch some company DVDs. That might be helpful at the time, but often things aren't quite the same in practice as in theory, are they? Most training courses are rather general and don't drill down to fit your specific context. A third option might be to have a mentor both to introduce you to a few other people and to let you shadow them. While this might be a great help for the first few days, you would probably soon feel awkward following them around all the time. At some point you have got to do your own job too!

So which option would you choose? Well, hopefully you wouldn't have to because a mixture of all three is what will train and equip you best. Being a Christian is way more exciting and radical than getting a new job. In fact, Jesus described it as an entirely new life! Just as we all needed help to grow up from babies to adults, so we all need help to grow up in our new life as Christians. That is what discipleship is: receiving personal help to become more like Jesus. Wow! Isn't that what we all long for?

Historically, Christian discipline has been divided into two categories – formative discipline and corrective discipline. 'Formative discipline helps to form the disciple through instruction. Corrective discipline helps to correct the disciple through correcting sin.'[1] When good parents teach and instruct their children they are 'disciplining' their children to follow a certain path. Corrective discipline is only used if their child strays and refuses to come back to the safe and good path. This is the same pattern for a healthy church family except we are all brothers and sisters.

In this chapter my aim is to explain what formative

---

1   Jonathan Leeman, *Church Discipline* (Crossway, 2012), 27.

discipline should look like. I shall use the more common term 'discipleship' to describe this aspect of church life. In the next chapter, Nigel will aim to explain what corrective discipline is and why that is sadly sometimes necessary.

Discipleship actually involves a wide spectrum of activities. It ranges from informal ad-hoc conversations between Christians through to more formal and intentional courses. Sometimes it could be a couple of women talking one to one about a specific issue but at other times it could be a church leader training a group of young men how to prepare and preach a sermon. But in all situations, the work of discipleship will be helping Christians to think and behave more like Jesus. More formally, a disciple is 'someone who submits to at least one other person in a healthy and appropriate way as a means of support and accountability'.[2] More generally, all church members are disciples who are slowly and steadily built up by the other members.

My main aim in this chapter is to persuade you to start or continue to grow a healthy culture of discipleship throughout your local church. But firstly, just what is the aim of discipleship?

The glorious aim of discipleship

In writing to the church in Ephesus, the apostle Paul describes their glorious future destiny of perfectly worshipping and enjoying fellowship with God in Jesus. He prayed that those

---

2   Bill Hull, *The Complete Book of Discipleship* (Navpress, 2006), 67.

believers would know this hope to which God had called them and the riches of their glorious inheritance. He wanted them to be thrilled not only by all that Christ had done, but also by what he was doing and would finally do for them all. 'And he [the Father] put all things under his [Christ, the Son's] feet and gave him as head over all things to the church, which is his body, the fullness of him who fills all in all' (Eph. 1:22-23).[3] And that is the vision for every local church too: to bask in the glory of worshipping our great God as we rule with him over all things in the new heaven and earth.

Having set such a great aim, Paul then moves on in his letter to remind the Ephesian believers that, as Christ's bride, a core part of their mission on earth was to prepare themselves for that coming day. We prepare for this by living more and more now as we will live perfectly then. Christ, by his Spirit, already lives within and among us now and so we have the privilege of enjoying communion with him and bringing our worship to him now. Your church has the great aim to be a community of praying, learning, growing, serving, giving, witnessing and joyfully worshipping believers. We are to do this together as a new, united people because of the unity the Holy Spirit brings. No longer are we to be divided by age or gender, race or class, relational status or personality type, educational qualification or tax code or whatever might have kept us apart. What a glorious vision for your local church!

However, it is painfully obvious that none of our churches is there yet. Even as individual believers we struggle to put

---

3   Scripture quotations in this chapter are ESV.

Christ first and to love even our Christian neighbours as ourselves. Yet, rather than fragment into a series of 'special interest churches' defined by external factors such as ethnic background or age, we are called to learn to build churches that bridge all our natural divides, living together as one united body. Rather than retreat as isolated individuals when we are hurt or struggle to connect with others, we are to embrace the awkward and essential challenge of our Christian community.[4] Therefore, the glorious aim of all discipleship is to equip ourselves to live together increasingly now as local churches with Christ as our head and our bridegroom. What an amazing project – to work together to build communities of heaven here on earth. What a beautiful task! But is discipleship really that important? Shouldn't the main aim of church-wide ministry be preaching the gospel to the lost?

The clear command for discipleship

After John 3:16, the 'Great Commission' verses of Matthew 28 are probably the next best-known verses of the New Testament: 'And Jesus came and said to them "All authority in heaven and on earth has been given to me. Go therefore and make disciples of all nations, baptising them in the name of the Father and of the Son and of the Holy Spirit, teaching them to observe all that I have commanded you. And behold, I am with you always, to the end of the age"' (Matt. 28:18-20). But here's the irony: they are also amongst the most misapplied.

---

4 Brett McCracken, *Uncomfortable* (Crossway, 2017).

To many people these verses are simply a call to evangelism. Yet they are a call to much more.

Jesus, the risen and vindicated Messiah King, was commanding his disciples to go and make disciples. Of course, making disciples starts with the preaching of the gospel, the call to repent and believe on Christ. Sinners need to be converted through the regenerating work of the Holy Spirit to become Christians. That's evangelism used by God.

Jesus' words did not stop there. Rather, he called them then to baptise these new disciples in the one name of the Father, Son and Holy Spirit. Becoming a Christian and remaining hidden is not enough: the command was to call them to a more public declaration of commitment in baptism as detailed in chapter three of this book. But do also see that Jesus' Great Commission is to even more than evangelism plus baptism. The burden of the call is, quite clearly, to make disciples through a life-long journey of obedience as these spiritually older disciples were to teach their spiritual juniors 'all that Jesus taught them.'

Ongoing discipleship therefore lies at the heart of the Great Commission, and so it is essential for all Christians both to be discipled and, to some degree, to be involved in discipling. But what are we to make of the phrase 'all that Jesus taught them'? If on the Emmaus road Jesus taught that all the Old Testament is about him, just where do we start?

The essential content of discipleship

Yes, the Bible is a big book, so it is easy to feel rather overwhelmed by our task. The apostle Paul told the Ephesian elders that he had not shrunk from declaring to them the 'whole counsel of God' (Acts 20:27). But just how do we do that? Well, although Paul must have summarised 'the whole counsel of God' in some balanced way, I want to commend to you two sets of three chapters that you could helpfully *start* with: Genesis 1-3 and Matthew 5-7.

Genesis 1-3 provides us with a clear biblical worldview. Therefore, these chapters provide the necessary foundational truths we need to 'make sense' of the rest of God's teaching. Just as we cannot fit the proverbial square peg in a round hole, neither can we fit the rest of the Bible's teaching into an atheistic or pantheistic worldview. In these opening chapters we can teach five foundational revelations about our world:

- *Genesis reveals God:* The 'I AM' – the one who has no beginning because he is eternal. Awesome! Ponder the wonder, the greatness and the majesty of God. We need to teach that the eternal and triune God is the main character in the whole universe.

- *Genesis reveals the world:* Created by God *ex nihilo* (from nothing). Our God spoke, and the universe was made! We need to teach that while all the universe is separate from God, it is completely dependent on God and ultimately belongs to him.

- *Genesis reveals mankind*: We need to teach that we are not animals but have been made in the image of God with dignity and creativity, having deep relationships and a morally responsible character that reflects the character of God. God made us and so we are not at liberty to recreate ourselves in a different image of our choosing.

- *Genesis reveals mankind's rebellion*: Without knowing this, we will never make sense of ourselves or the gospel. We have followed our ancestors' path and branded God irrelevant and will naturally worship anyone and anything instead. This explains the mess and pain around and within us. Our sin has ruined the good creation of God.

- *Gloriously, Genesis also reveals just a glimpse of God's salvation*: How exciting to discover that the first promise of the gospel was given in the fallout of mankind's rebellion! How wonderful to see that Satan was told that Jesus would come from the seed of Eve to crush his head while he attempted to bruise Jesus' heel.

Can I encourage you to make sure you intentionally disciple all new Christians and members in these foundational truths? Without a clear understanding of these truths, much of the rest of the Bible will seem rather arbitrary to them. With them, the glorious big picture of the gospel will become clear.

Foundations need to be built on. So can I suggest you also include the Sermon on the Mount from Matthew 5-7 in your core discipleship plan? Because here, Jesus gave his 'Kingdom Manifesto' to explain how we Christians are to live, and as he taught his disciples to teach others all he taught them, he must surely have had this in mind.[5]

The Sermon on the Mount is such a rich and helpful summary of the Christian life. It starts with an awesome assurance that, because we have already been saved and brought into the kingdom, we are accepted and blessed by God. Even our struggles to become more like Jesus will lead to more blessings. Yes, trouble may come as we live holy yet active lives as salt and light but even that will be used to bless outsiders with the gospel. The sermon continues with the call to show true righteousness in contrast to the hypocrisy of the Pharisees. Who on earth can achieve this? No one without Christ's righteousness objectively given to them and without Christ's Spirit subjectively working within them. We must ensure that this never seems like earning salvation, but the fruit of the Spirit applying Christ's saving work within us.

Jesus then taught about several down-to-earth topics such as anger, lust, divorce, oath taking, retaliation, love and giving. How practical! How challenging! Of course, we are always going to need help, so the sermon continues with a lesson on prayer. Jesus taught a wonderful truth: we Christians have been adopted and so are able to call God our Father. What a wonderful privilege to cry out to him! Where are we to start? With him and the honour of his name and the growth of his kingdom. Only then does the prayer turn to us with the needs of our bodies, the forgiveness of our sins and protection for our souls.

---

5   I am thankful to Phil Heaps for making this observation.

Following prayer, Jesus taught about the need to be entirely loyal to God and for him to be our treasure such that we are freed from anxiety and regret. What challenging words! Yet, what comforting words too. Chapter 7 finishes the discipleship course with teaching not to be judgmental yet to be discerning, the golden rule and the reality of the narrow way of Christ.

Of course, Genesis 1-3 and Matthew 5-7 are not the sum total of discipleship. Other core passages include Romans 3-6, Ephesians 4-6, and Philippians 2-3. Hopefully these can help you make a start with more formal discipleship teaching.

The Puritans encouraged the use of catechisms together with instruction in the Ten Commandments and the Lord's Prayer.[6] The book you are holding can be a helpful resource too. Why not plan to read and discuss it with someone else? At the end of the book are also listed just a few of the many other good discipleship resources you can use. But here is the danger: by writing about certain Bible passages and discipleship courses I must not give the impression that discipleship is merely an intellectual exercise in reading and Bible study. It cannot be less than that, but it should also be *much* more. So, what is the best method for doing discipleship?

---

6   J. I. Packer and G. A. Parrett, *Grounded in the Gospel* (Baker Books, 2010).

The best method for discipleship

Marshall McLuhan coined the now popular phrase 'The medium is the message'[7] What he meant was that the way in which a message is communicated (the medium) has a profound effect on that message. He was right. Therefore, we need to realise that the way in which we 'do discipleship' also matters. Merely seeing discipleship as a series of accurate Bible studies encourages a more cerebral view of the Christian life than is healthy and therefore runs the risk of missing a crucial aspect of Christlikeness.

We can learn the best method by looking at how Jesus discipled his own disciples. He called them to a shared life with him. He did not select them based on some ideal social mix, as they were from varied backgrounds and had radically different temperaments. Nor did he choose them for their sharp minds or deep pockets. We need to learn to apply the same approach today: we Christians from all backgrounds need to be taught together in a shared life.

Sometimes Jesus taught his disciples through structured discourses, but much of their time was spent travelling, eating and visiting different places. All this was a rich time of watching Jesus and his reactions to others and learning how he answered tough questions. As they shared their lives together, something of the character and behaviour of Jesus rubbed off on them.

---

7   Marshall McLuhan and Quentin Fiore, *The Medium is the Message* (Penguin, 1967).

Jesus' call to make disciples is far more than a call to do one-to-one Bible studies. It is also a call to live radically different lives in front of others, so that our character and integrity will validate our message. It is a call to invite others to learn by listening, by asking, by watching us live our own Christian lives. Perhaps the closest equivalent we have to this today is army training where small groups learn far more than how to operate machinery! Each unit of soldiers learns how to live as a team and follow important instructions. How should we 'do discipleship'? Like Jesus, within the context of a shared life.

Of course, that might sound all well and good, but just how practical is this? Surely, I am not expecting you to provide continuous 'weekend retreats'? Well, no I'm not, because in his wisdom, Jesus has already established a far more workable and affordable arena for a shared life: your local church.

The best context for discipleship

If Matthew 28:18-20 can be called our 'mission statement' then Ephesians 4 is to be our 'method statement.' We are to live out our lives as Christians as members of local churches. This has already been argued for earlier in this book. But here I want you to see that each local church is also the ideal place for a shared life that generates purposeful discipleship. Paul writes:

> And he gave the apostles, the prophets, the evangelists, the shepherds and teachers, to equip the saints for the work of

ministry, for building up the body of Christ, until we all attain to the unity of the faith and of the knowledge of the Son of God, to mature manhood, to the measure of the stature of the fullness of Christ, so that we may no longer be children, tossed to and fro by the waves and carried about by every wind of doctrine, by human cunning, by craftiness in deceitful schemes. Rather, speaking the truth in love, we are to grow up in every way into him who is the head, into Christ, from whom the whole body, joined and held together by every joint with which it is equipped, when each part is working properly, makes the body grow so that it builds itself up in love. (Eph. 4:11-16)

Paul explains that pastors and teachers have not been given to local churches simply to do all the ministry themselves. Rather, they have been given to equip all the other members to serve in ministry as well. As has already been argued in this book, when people become Christians they are to be baptised and join a local church community. But then what? The great aim, as we have already seen, is to grow more like Christ, and this is achieved by the mutual love and care other members of our church show us as they speak the truth in love. Just as the African proverb says that it takes a village to raise a child, so it takes a church to grow every disciple!

How do younger Christians learn what it is like to be a godly father or mother? By older Christians discipling them through example and instruction. All those meals together also provide the opportunity to see parenting in action. That is the clear teaching of Titus 2. How best can a church serve a young mum? By an older mum coming alongside her with practical help and teaching in a shared life. All those chats over coffee can provide support and practical wisdom. How can our senior saints be helped and encouraged? By the friendship of younger members who serve and care. When people pop around to play Scrabble or do housework this also provides the context for many other forms of support. Do you see? The very life of a healthy local church is the naturally shared life.

At the time of the Reformation 500 years ago, Martin Luther rediscovered what is often termed 'the priesthood of all believers.' This was the biblical teaching that the church members are together a royal priesthood with everyone Spirit-equipped to play a useful part (see 1 Peter 2:5). This was a radical thing when church life had been sharply separated between laity and clergy. Yet we need to fight not to return to that idea in more subtle ways. We need to resist the temptation to widen the gap between the 'ministry team' and other members. We need to be careful not to professionalise ministry. Yes, discipling includes teaching, but it also includes living everyday shared lives where various effects of the gospel are lived out and supported by the life of each local church. This was Paul's encouragement to the church in Rome: 'I myself am satisfied about you, my brothers, that you yourselves are full of goodness, filled with all knowledge and able to instruct one another' (Rom. 15:14). Are you encouraged to see that your local church – however big or small – is the context for your discipleship? Your church is where it's at!

Barriers to a culture of discipleship

Sadly, not every local church has a healthy culture of discipleship. Often this explains why some are in decline. Put bluntly: a failure to disciple is effectively a plan to die out! Why do some churches lack a culture of discipleship? Here are four possible barriers.

Firstly, there can be a lack of leadership in this area. Whilst church growth needs to be organic, it also needs some structure and leadership. Much as we tend to parent as we were parented, so church leaders tend to follow subconsciously the example they were given. Yet some of the most committed and effective leader-disciplers I know were intentionally discipled themselves. They have told me how, as younger Christians, certain people committed to invest in them. Praise the Lord! Not only were they helped to grow, but they became both convinced and equipped to go and do likewise. If that has not been your experience, perhaps you need to take a conscious decision to change and lead more in this area.

Secondly, there can be a mistaken view that pulpit preaching is sufficient to disciple. After all, if we believe in the sufficiency of Scripture and the power of preaching, then people will be built up in their faith simply by hearing good expository preaching, won't they? Of course, there is a lot of truth in this, but while expository preaching rightly addresses and applies each specific text, it cannot always deal with all the other questions, problems and issues that different people have. How long might it be before new

Christians encounter teaching on the specific issues they are facing? While preaching must form the backbone of church life, a more tailored and individual discipleship ministry is also needed. Even the apostle Paul who called Timothy to preach the word to the Christians in Ephesus (2 Tim. 4:2) had previously gone house to house teaching the new believers (Acts 20:20). Discipleship is not about replacing preaching but giving additional tailored teaching.

Thirdly, there can be over-formality in church life. Whilst gathering for organised services of worship is vital, it must not be the sum total of church life, or we will fail to get close to each other and develop a shared life where opportunities for discipleship can flourish. Some members (even pastors) may prefer mere formality if they struggle with social interaction. Some may have been badly wounded by experiences of 'heavy shepherding' where pastors have overstepped their role. Some may be wracked with unresolved guilt over past sins and worry about others finding out. All these things will work against a healthy culture of discipleship yet removing them may take much time and patience. Over-formality can be removed slowly through adjusting service formats, encouraging informal times after services (especially shared meals) and by using homes as venues for some meetings. Fear of abuse or condemnation can be removed as leaders display love and kindness in sharing their own worries and troubles too. A shared life ought to work both ways with leaders becoming vulnerable, like Paul who was willing to share his life: 'So, being affectionately desirous of you, we were ready to share with you not only the gospel of God but also our own selves, because you had become very dear to us' (1 Thess. 2:8).

Fourthly, the sin of laziness can be another barrier. None of what I have written will be easy to apply. Therefore, we need to pray for a culture of persistent hard work if we are going to progress in developing a healthy culture of church discipleship. People change very slowly, so we always have to play the long game. Don't we know that in ourselves? In addition to our own tendency to laziness, we may well encounter apathy amongst some members if they fail to see the need for discipleship. After all, they believe the gospel, don't they? Isn't that enough?

We live in a culture that celebrates expressive individualism and so living deeply shared lives in a church is counter-cultural. It will require a gradual change in habits and it will require clear commitments. We need to press upon us all the biblical exhortation to work hard rather than to coast towards heaven. Paul wrote to the Colossian believers:

> Christ we proclaim, warning everyone and teaching everyone with all wisdom, that we may present everyone mature in Christ. For this I toil, struggling with all his energy that he powerfully works within me. (Col. 1:28-29)

With the Lord's help these barriers to discipleship can and will be lowered and removed. A culture of discipleship flourishes where a growing number of church members mature and catch the vision to be equipped to disciple others themselves (see Col. 2:6-7). Through the modelling of the local church leaders more people will catch the vision. It is a positive case of pyramid selling! And therefore, the multiplication of disciplers will enable your church to grow and stay strong. My hope in this chapter has been to encourage you to take up this challenge with joy.

What might a discipleship culture look like?

I hope I have persuaded you that your church both needs and can have a healthy culture of discipleship. It will be the pathway to becoming a church community where Christ delights to dwell by his Spirit. Picture these practical examples of how this culture of discipleship might look as it grows in your church:

- There is a buzz of conversation and co-operation in the now monthly fellowship meals on the first Sunday of the month. Most members take the initiative to welcome visitors, who sense a real spirit of love amongst the people. More come early to the meetings in order to serve others. That's applying Hebrews 10:23-24 in a practical way.

- A young lady hears about the remarkable conversion story of an older member and volunteers to help her write it up to encourage other believers and be a tool for evangelism. Their friendship across the generations helps both of them to grow and deepens their love for each other (Col. 4:8).

- A relatively new couple in the church become keen to show practical love. They take the initiative to invite a disabled church member over for dinner and keep a look out for others whom they can serve. As they invite different combinations of people, so new friendships develop – putting Romans 12:13 into action.

- A middle-aged mum invites various other mums over for coffee both to study the word and to pray. At various times questions about marriage and parenting come up and biblical support is given. Out of all this, some of them decide to form a regular ladies' home Bible study group. This is Titus 2:3-4 in a modern setting.

- A few men decide to go out regularly for breakfast and this turns into a book reading group. Eventually other men join and read and discuss a chapter of a book once a month. Various friendships and support networks develop and new avenues of service develop (1 Thess. 5:11).

- An older member falls ill and spends time in hospital. On hearing this, the various members whom she has encouraged and supported are moved to visit her and pray with her. One of the nurses asks who all these people are! That's John 13:34 in action.

- After some unwise words on social media, a few people courageously decide to talk and pray together after the church service. Acting on Matthew 18:15 restores fellowship.

- At a church members' meeting there is a sweet display of unity in the pursuit of a brother who has left to follow unorthodox teaching. In the end a few men volunteer to go and visit him. They eventually support the sad need to remove him from membership. Following Matthew 18:15-17 they keep the church pure.

- The number of people attending the Lord's Supper grows as they see this as both a means of grace and an opportunity to reaffirm the unity of the church in Christ. They're catching a foretaste of Revelation 19:9.

These are just a few ways in which a culture of discipleship and mutual support might grow in your church. I hope you will be encouraged as you see such things flourishing.

Conclusion

Congratulations, you've got the job! But how will you be trained and equipped to do it?

I hope I have persuaded you that every Christian has useful work to do in the kingdom of our Lord. We are all priests who serve in the new covenant temple. Yet we all need to be trained and equipped for our different tasks. Wonderfully, the Lord has provided us all that we need in the Bible and the best support networks in each of our local churches.

Can you see what your role is? Are you quietly beavering away helping others to see theirs and flourish in their callings? Your local church *can* be characterised by a shared life of discipleship. As all the members are equipped, they will be encouraged to use their gifts to serve others in various works of ministry and prayer. What an amazing blessing to be part of a community where God is at work! What an exciting business to be equipping people to grow to serve Christ and his people! What an awesome privilege to be members of Christ's embassies who shine out the effects of his marvellous gospel of grace!

Together, may our local churches be even purer and brighter displays of heaven on earth.

Questions for discussion

1. Why could Genesis 1-3 and Matthew 5-7 be useful Bible passages to teach new believers?
2. What else did Jesus do to disciple his disciples in addition to teaching?
3. Why is the local church the best context for your discipleship growth?
4. How might a healthy culture of discipleship be hindered in a local church? How could this affect the long-term health of the church?
5. Look again at the practical examples of a shared life of discipleship in the local church. What evidences of a healthy culture of discipleship do you see in your church that you can be thankful for? How can you play your part and build up the body of Christ going forwards?

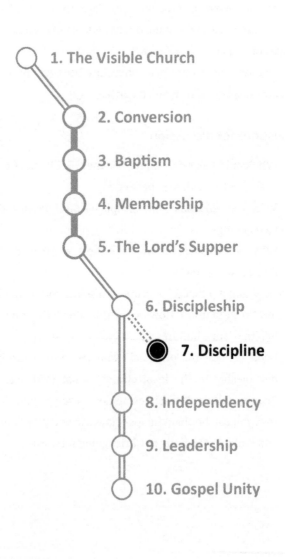

1. The Visible Church

2. Conversion

3. Baptism

4. Membership

5. The Lord's Supper

6. Discipleship

7. Discipline

8. Independency

9. Leadership

10. Gospel Unity

7. Discipline

The corrective action when members stray

Nigel Graham

7. *We believe that church discipline is a provision of Christ for the protection of the honour of his name in a local church. This removal from church membership, and withholding of the Lord's Supper, may become necessary against any church member whose life or doctrine renders their profession of faith in Christ incredible. It is used after much pastoral care, and in order that the offender might be brought back to repentance and faith, and afterwards gladly readmitted to church membership.*

Hands were raised. Not all, but a majority. D was 'excommunioned' from C Baptist Church. D would not repent of his ongoing open sexual sinning. A few members had said, 'Give him more time'. A few said, 'Don't be unkind. Who of us is perfect?' But the vast majority knew it had gone on too long. D was not representing Jesus well. So they expelled him from the membership. Wow, they felt so awful. So cruel.

The kind mum lovingly doses her child with disgusting medicine so that the child gets better. The kind surgeon lovingly (painfully!) removes a cancerous growth, so that the patient lives – and the cancer doesn't spread. The kind teacher lovingly corrects your maths mistakes, so that you'll (theoretically!) learn, and pass the future exam. The kind headteacher lovingly – reluctantly – excludes the violent pupil so that the other pupils are safe and the school's reputation is untarnished.

Kind, loving, restorative, painful, healing, lifesaving, corrective, protective discipline is part of a healthy family, healthy school, healthy society. It's also part of a healthy church. A kind and loving part.

What is church discipline?

In its widest sense, church discipline is helping one another to be holier, to become mature in Jesus (Eph. 4:12-16). A church is a group sanctification pilgrimage (Heb. 3:12-13). We are lovingly assisting each other to make it to the new creation in as good a shape as possible.

Historically, discipline has been divided into two categories – formative discipline and corrective discipline. 'Formative discipline helps to form the disciple through instruction. Corrective discipline helps to correct the disciple through correcting sin.'[1] Formative discipline is incredibly important and was the subject of the previous chapter. This chapter will focus on corrective discipline.

1 Jonathan Leeman, *Church Discipline* (Crossway, 2012), 27. I acknowledge my indebtedness to Leeman's studies.

Correcting sin inside the church will most often happen informally and privately. But if a member doesn't respond to these more informal corrections, then the final endgame is the involuntary ending of their membership. If baptism/membership is the front door of the church, then church discipline is the back door of the church. The individual is no longer identified with the Lord's church. The individual can no longer participate in the Lord's Supper. This can be called 'excommunication', which is just another way of saying, 'ex-communion-ing'.

In this narrow sense then, church discipline is a church's act of removing a church member from church membership and the withholding of the Lord's Supper from them.

A church should hold its Bible open and say, 'We must obey this.' A church with a heart full of kindness says, 'We will make this painful declaration because we love Christ, the church, the offender and the world.' So, in this narrow sense, church discipline is a formal, public declaration. In loving concern, a church says to one of its members, 'Because of your present behaviour and/or belief, we don't think your profession of faith is credible. With the authority invested in us by Christ, we therefore remove our affirmation of your profession of faith.'

Why do we not really like church discipline?

Let's face it, to the average Western mind, church discipline doesn't sell well. It doesn't sound good.

What right has a bunch of imperfect people to pry into

the lives of other imperfect people? How dare you make pronouncements about the beliefs and/or behaviour of other imperfect people? Church discipline sounds medieval, judgmental, arrogant and basically just nasty. Certainly not loving.

Church discipline doesn't sell well to many genuine believers and gospel churches. Abuses of the practice make us very nervous. Who of us wants a church where we're all poking our noses into each other's personal lives? We hear stories of unfair cases, maybe spiritual abuse, and we don't want to go there.

We are nervous because many advocates of church discipline seem to focus on the 'big sins', whilst often ignoring the respectable 'sin planks' in their own eyes. It seems to be about getting rid of the sexually sinning member quickly, whilst turning a blind eye to the divisive deacon (apologies to deacons!) or the grousing granny (apologies to grannies!).

Misuses of Bible texts lead to some Christians becoming wary of church discipline. 'Didn't Jesus say we shouldn't judge others?' (referencing Matt. 7:1-2). 'All sin is the same. How can I correct your adultery when I lust? Didn't Jesus say lust is adultery?' (referencing Matt. 5:28). 'Surely, love should overlook a brother's sin?' (1 Pet. 4:8). Such misinterpretations become evangelical folklore, accepted as Bible truth, meaning that whilst Bible believers don't actively oppose church discipline, there is often a very real reluctance to practise it, grounded in a conviction that it's not really the best way. Sadly, even Bible-believing Christians can say or suggest, 'I know it says we should do discipline in the Bible, but...'

Hyper-individualism infects our Western churches, especially more traditional evangelical churches. Piety is personal. We live hyper-privatised Christian lives. We never really open our lives to other members. This makes church discipline seem like snooping.

The very nature and make up of many churches puts us off doing church discipline. In smaller churches, we all know each other so well. We become close friends. The very thought of doing church discipline to our friends sends shivers down our spines. 'I just can't do it.' Add the further complication of blood family ties in many churches. Blood is often thicker than the Holy Spirit. Blood ties can blind us to even the most blatant sins.

Many churches, maybe younger and newer churches, do one-to-one corrective discipline amazingly well (applying Matt. 18:15). Therefore, they don't really see the need to emphasise and practise the more corporate whole-church aspects of discipleship. This can be linked with a subtle gospel reductionism, which hints that church discipline is too time consuming and too formal. Let's get on with spreading the gospel to the lost and cultivating disciples informally.

Yet saying all this, all of us have a deep sense that corrective discipline is necessary in many walks of life. Referees carry red cards. Companies fire employees. Corrective discipline is needed in the church for unrepented sin.

What is the purpose of church discipline?

Once you merely assume the purpose of church discipline, you will soon lose the practice of church discipline. If we don't start with the why, church discipline will die. Perhaps we should have started this chapter with the 'why?' (though it was helpful to stop to define the terms and fend off the brickbats!).

The church is important to God. The church is at the centre of God's redemptive plan in Christ (Eph. 1:22; 3:10-11, 21).[2] And the only place where the church is made visible is the local church. So how a local church functions matters to him. 'Who is in the church?' and 'who is out of the church?' matters.

Church discipline is lovingly given by Christ to the church for which he died, for a number of purposes.[3] I'm going for four here.[4]

These four purposes are organised around a word you're possibly not expecting – love. It's vital to look through these 'love lenses' as we think about 'why bother with church discipline?'

Love for Jesus

The good name and honour of Jesus Christ demands that his church should be kept pure. If God's name was blasphemed

2   Jeremy Kimble, 40 Questions about Church Membership and Discipline (Kregel, 2017), 16-17.

3   For an outstanding overview of the subject see Wayne Grudem, Systematic Theology (IVP, 1994), 894-901.

4   Jonathan Leeman, Church Membership (Crossway, 2012), 110-111.

when the Jews dishonoured God (Rom. 2:24), how much more if a new covenant member dishonours Christ? Every member of the team body represents the team head. A holy bridegroom's reputation is dirtied if his bride is unholy (Eph. 5:27). Jesus is jealous for his own honour (Rev. 2:14-15, 20). So must we be.

Love for the church

Sin contaminates. Sin spreads (1 Cor. 5:2, 6-7). When sin is not sorted out, sin spreads like yeast in dough or cancer in the body. So the church needs protection from the toxic spread of sin (Heb. 12:14-15).

When a church takes the holiness of one of its members seriously, it is saying to the other members that sin is serious. 'Unrepented of' sin damages and ultimately leads to hell. In Corinth, Paul warns baptised, believing 'belongers' that anyone can fall (1 Cor. 10:1-13). Correcting sins promotes perseverance. When any secular organisation has to fairly yet firmly discipline and remove a member, the existing members feel warned about their own conduct and are all put on their toes. Correcting sins warns other church members (Deut. 17:12-13; 1 Tim. 5:19-20). And warnings are loving.

Love for the offender

A loving parent screams 'Stop!' as she sees her child crossing the road into oncoming traffic. Church discipline is God screaming 'Stop!' to a straying child. It might sound and seem harsh and nasty. In truth it is kind and loving.

Fatherly corrective discipline is God's way of loving his sinning children (Heb. 12:1-14). God loves a sinning believer too much to not bring short-term pain for long-term gain (Heb. 12:10-11). So if we want to love like God does, we will use this loving gift of Christ's to try to restore the offender. A loving church is one which will lovingly discipline one of its members to bring about repentance. A hating church is one which won't discipline one of its members (Prov. 13:24). 'Gaining your brother/sister' is the goal (Matt. 18:15). Restoring them is the purpose (Gal. 6:1). Our goals are repentance, restoration and reconciliation.

It is painful to correct someone. It hurts all involved. Who of us enjoys awkward conversations and tense meetings? But in the process of church discipline, and even in the final step of 'ex-communion-ing', a church is lovingly saying to a person, 'You're heading for hell. We beg you. Stop. Turn. Repent. It's not too late' (1 Tim. 1:20; 1 Cor. 5:5).

Love for the world

The world is watching your church – as a city on a hill (Matt. 5:13). The world expects Christians to be sincere and better behaved than them. When church members behave like their non-Christian friends (and worse) and nothing is done about it, our evangelistic edge is blunted. In Corinth, the behaviour of a church member was worse than the behaviour of non-Christians – and the church was doing nothing about it (1 Cor. 5:1-2). A church which sensitively and seriously deals with sin in its ranks, teaches the world that sin is serious, that sincerity matters, that Christians don't brush dirt under the carpet (Phil. 2:15). Regular attenders are loved if we show them that membership demands a certain level of behaviour and belief.

When should a church practise church discipline?

Rarely! When necessary!

All sin is serious. All sin needs correcting. All sin requires rebuking and repenting of. In a healthy Christian, much of this correcting is self-correcting. Self-correction may come from the Scriptures, from conscience, from sermons, from the example of others. Sometimes our sins will need tender correcting by others. This may well be by simple, subtle questions. Sometimes some sins may need more direct correcting, but still privately and informally. A healthy church has an atmosphere of loving transparency where members love and trust each other so much, they are happy to receive and give gentle correction (though in a hyper-privatised culture this is easier said than done!). Oh for churches where all of us are desperate to help each other to repent of our sins.

But when and for what should this loving and tender but more formal and public discipline take place? Any sin? Every sin?

The list approach

A common approach for churches is to seek to list the sins for which we should move to formal discipline. But the fact is that the Bible does not give us hard and fast lists of which sins should put you on the church discipline schedule. Some examples in Scripture are 'divisiveness (Rom. 16:17; Titus 3:10), incest (1 Cor. 5:1), laziness and refusing to work (2 Thess. 3:6-10), disobeying what Paul writes (2 Thess. 3:14-15), blasphemy (1 Tim. 1:20) and teaching heretical doctrine (2 John 10-11)'.[5] And these are surely given as examples, rather than as an exclusive list.

The credibility approach

Is there an approach which moves away from the list mentality – that is more theologically nuanced, that is truer to the biblical materials and which allows room for pastoral and situational sensitivity? Jonathan Leeman argues for such an approach. 'This is the "gospel framework" approach to discipline ... It is not driven by lists of which sins qualify for discipline. It is driven by the single question of whether a church can continue to publicly affirm a person's profession of faith as credible.'[6]

The key issue is this: Is your profession of faith still credible, given your current behaviour and/or belief?

Since each gospel church has been given the authority by Christ to *affirm* a disciple's profession of faith (Matt. 16:13-20; 18:15-20), each gospel church has been given the authority by Christ to *remove* that affirmation of a person's profession of

---

5   Grudem, *Systematic Theology*, 896.

6   Leeman, *Church Discipline*, 49.

faith. The key issue is credibility. We baptise anyone with a credible profession of faith. We can get it wrong, but we open the door into church membership on the basis of this credible profession of faith. Church discipline can only take place and must take place when a member's belief or behaviour lacks credibility – when the profession on their lips becomes unbelievable because of what they claim to believe or because of their behaviour. We open the back door of the church to a person whose profession is no longer credible. We could be wrong. We are not saying you are definitely not a Christian. We are simply saying, 'We just can't affirm your profession anymore' (1 Cor. 5:12-13).

Just as baptism is a church giving a believer the 'Jesus team jersey' to wear, so church discipline is saying, 'We can't continue to say you're on the Jesus team. You seem to be playing for the opposition (1 Cor. 5:5; Matt. 18:17). We're taking your team jersey off. We're going to regard you as wearing the opposition jersey. But, we are desperate for you to return to the Jesus team.'

For what type of sins

So what sins cause someone to lose credibility in the church's eyes? What sin is it that, left uncorrected, gives the lie to a Christian's profession? In the 1800s, in a Cambridgeshire church, a man was disciplined for dancing in his parlour! It is crucial that we only call sin what the Bible calls sin. We are not to use our own cultural taboos to impose discipleship. Wouldn't it be convenient if the Bible neatly compartmentalised sins for us, into an 'overlook these foibles' column (I'm pretty sure we'd put 'dancing in the parlour' in that column!), a 'keep working on that character trait' column, and an 'alarm flashing; not compatible with credible profession of faith' column?!

Leeman helpfully describes three features of a sin which may help a church to ascertain whether a person has lost credibility. All three must be generally present, but this is not an exact science, nor a tick list. Leeman calls it, 'Sins we don't expect in a Christian.'[7]

- *Outward sin.* Under the old covenant, witnesses were needed to give evidence in court. Outward sins were punished. So in the new covenant, the sin must be outward too. There must be evidence. One needs to see sin and hear sin before one thinks of church discipline. Churches must never operate a 'thought police' mentality. We're talking public and provable sins before public discipline is warranted.

- *Serious sin.* All sin is serious. But not all sins are as serious as others. Not all sins are the same as other sins. Under the old covenant not all sins were disciplined by exclusion from the camp. Lust was sin, but only adultery was punishable by death. In the church, not all sins are disciplined by exclusion from the church. Lust is still sin. But lust is not the same as fornication. The quarrellers in Corinth (1 Cor. 1:11) are not (yet?) in the same boat as the sexually immoral man (1 Cor. 5:1ff). Doctrinal deviations

---

7 Leeman, *Church Discipline*, 47-65.

must be serious, not secondary, to warrant church discipline.

- *'Unrepented of' sin.* Repentance – or the lack of it – is mega. You don't remove repentant sinners from the church. But, if a person refuses to repent of a sinful belief or behaviour, then discipline must occur. Characteristic unrepentance is not the mark of a believer. Habitual unrepentance is not the team jersey Christians wear. Repentance is not remorse or regret that I've been caught (2 Cor. 7:8-12). This issue is vital and complex. How do we know if someone is truly repentant? Is a simple 'sorry' enough? Again it's that credibility word. Is their repentance credible? A truly repentant person offers no excuses, blames only themselves and is willing to take the discipline, whatever it is.[8] Paul's gospel was that sinners must repent, turn to God and demonstrate their repentance by their deeds (Acts 26:20). Sometimes repentance and the test of credible repentance may come after 'ex-communion-ing' has already taken place (as appears to have been the case in the quickie discipline of 1 Cor. 5). Often, thankfully, repentance and the test of credible repentance takes place in the process of confrontation and correction (as in Matt. 18:13-19). Pastoral care and pastoral sensitivity are fundamental. Even the same sin in two members might be treated differently, dependent on maturity and circumstances (Jude 22-23).

---

8   Three Old Testament kings. Saul made excuses (1 Sam. 15). Solomon couldn't see it (1 Kgs. 11). Only David truly repented (2 Sam. 12).

How does a church implement church discipline?

Remember, the issue is correcting sin in the church. Remember, the 'love purposes' are the honour of Christ, the protection of the church's purity, the restoration of the offender and the good name of Christ in the world. The aim is to bring the offender to repentance, restoration and reconciliation. The aim is for the church to forgive.

For a full picture on how to implement church discipline, we need to synthesise the two major passages (Matt.18:15-19; 1 Cor. 5:1-13) and many other New Testament passages (Rom. 16:17-18; Gal. 6:1; 1 Thess. 5:14; 2 Thess. 3:6-15; 2 Tim. 3:5; Titus 3:10; 2 John 10).

The process

Here is the sad situation. A member seems to have sinned or to be sinning. It's sin that cannot be overlooked. It seems to be serious, outward and 'unrepented of'. Matthew 18:15-20 gives members a flexible process to work through with sensitivity.

A key principle of church discipline is that the process of correcting sin must involve as few people as necessary.[9]

Firstly, we begin with one-to-one confrontation (Matt. 18:15), hoping this will lead to repentance.

Secondly, if this loving private confrontation is unsuccessful, then take a select few (Matt. 18:16) and lovingly urge repentance.

Thirdly, if there is still no repentance, the whole church

---

9 Leeman, *Church Discipline*, 68.

must be informed (Matt. 18:17b). Pastoral wisdom, sensitivity and flexibility will be needed in terms of time scales, leaving time between members' meetings for the offender to realise the seriousness of his sin and, hopefully, repenting.

Finally, if there is still no credible repentance to the church, then this person must be excluded by the gathered church (1 Cor. 5:1-5) from the membership and from the Lord's Table (1 Cor. 5:11) and treated as an unbeliever (Matt. 18:17b; 1 Cor. 5:9-13).

In the other pivotal passage (1 Cor. 5:1-13) Paul commands the church to exclude quickly. This is possibly because it seems the sin is very serious, the sin is very outward and the sinner is very unrepentant! Sometimes speed is of the essence. The Bible gives flexibility.[10]

The elder (leaders)

Somewhere in this process, perhaps after one-to-one confrontation has failed, the elders of the church get involved – more than involved. As ones who will give an account (Heb. 13:17) and who care for the church (Acts 20:28), they will be leading the process. Elders admonish and care (1 Thess. 5:12; Titus 1:9, 13). Elders will need to shepherd members through such a difficult time. But it is abundantly clear that

---

10 If through this process, the church member wishes to avoid the threat of corrective discipline by resigning, then for everyone's good, don't let them. A person cannot 'member' themselves, so they cannot 'unmember' themselves. See Leeman, Church Discipline, 117. For a longer discussion, see https://www.9marks.org/article/preemptive-resignation-get-out-jail-free-card [accessed 11-11-21].

it is the church membership that has been given authority to remove and exclude (Matt. 18:17; 1 Cor. 5:2-5).

Suspension

Many excellent churches include suspension of membership privileges in the process of church discipline. Suspension is a serious formal act of warning, often barring a sinning member from the Lord's Supper and other privileges, in the hope that this will promote repentance. The pivotal passage used to support suspension is 2 Thessalonians 3:6-15, especially verses 14-15: 'Take special note of anyone who does not obey our instruction in this letter. Do not associate with them, in order that they may feel ashamed. Yet do not regard them as an enemy, but warn them as you would a fellow believer.'[11]

Stopping someone having the members' meal is surely *de facto* removal from membership. 2 Thessalonians 3 is not speaking of suspension but of excommunication.[12] Paul has already exhorted members to warn sinning believers (1 Thess. 5:14; 2 Thess. 3:6). 2 Thessalonians 3:14-15 is the end of the process. He is using the same 'excommunication language' as 1 Corinthians 5, even using the same verb, 'associate' (1 Cor. 5:9, 11). 'Warn him as you would a fellow believer' means that the 'brotherly' demeanour and tone of our rebukes will

---

11 Scripture quotations in this chapter are NIV; for a comprehensive treatment of all the views on this verse in relation to church discipline, see Greg Beale, *1-2 Thessalonians* (IVP, 2003), 260-264.

12 I am now more inclined to the view that the suspension of membership privileges seems to be foreign to the rest of Scripture.

be different than if he had never been a member and always been a pagan! Beale writes, "'warn him as a brother", such that continued unrepentance means that he may not, indeed, be a true Christian. Thus, there is an intentional ambivalence about how the person is to be treated and regarded.'[13]

This view means that we would not add another formal layer of discipline called 'suspension of privileges'. Let's maybe have more informal private warnings, elder warnings, letter warnings and church members' meeting warnings, and loving warnings that you will be 'ex-communion-ed' if you don't repent.

The treatment of the excluded person

If a church takes the sad step of removal from membership, other members are often confused about how to treat the excluded person? Are we Amish? What's shunning?

Leeman offers excellent biblical counsel on how to treat disciplined individuals: 'the general tenor of one's relationships with the disciplined individual should markedly change. Interactions should not be characterised by casualness but by deliberate conversations about repentance. Certainly family members should continue to fulfil family obligations (Eph. 6:1-3; 1 Tim. 5:8; 1 Peter 3:1-2)'.[14] The disciplined person must ordinarily be welcomed to come to the services. That's where they will hear the word

---

13 Beale, 1-2 Thessalonians, 263.

14 Leeman, Church Membership, 115.

and hopefully repent. (Though sometimes for safeguarding reasons, it may be more appropriate for the person to attend another church's services.)

Restoration of the offender

Sadly, we often act as though the goal of church discipline is to make a problem – or a problem person! – go away. The reverse should be true. Our hearts' desire must be for repentance, restoration and reconciliation. Once the credibility of the repentance is evidenced (and this is sometimes ... often ... complicated) then full and free forgiveness must be given (Matt. 18:21ff).

Restoration means restoration to membership and the Lord's Supper, because the church now affirms their profession of faith – it's credible. The church will joyfully give a formal and public declaration of forgiveness and love (2 Cor. 2:5-8). What rejoicing! This loving gift of Christ has done its work. The sinner is restored, the church has been warned, Christ's good name has been honoured!

Restoration may not be easy and it may well require specific teaching from church leaders to prepare and guide church members through this process. By restoring a repentant member well, the church is able to demonstrate the grace of the gospel in a very tangible way.

Conclusion

God gives us principles to apply wisely. We are not told

how quickly or slowly these procedures should take place. Surely calm investigation of evidence (Deut. 19:18) and careful listening to people are demanded – with much prayer, because these issues are complex. Love is needed because we often act in revenge. Courage is needed because we may have to offend and we will have to make decisions. We must walk towards the pain and not hope things will sort themselves out. We will need to be aware of, and beware of, cowardice cloaked in compassion and of second-guessing consequences. We will need to do what is right, leaving the results in God's hands.

The culture of the church that will practise church discipline properly

The nuts and bolts are important. Procedures are vital. Different cases will be handled differently.[15] But the pervading atmosphere and culture of a church are fundamental if church discipline is going to be embraced and seen as a loving gift to be used – rarely but where necessary. What will such a church culture look like? What mood music will prevent sin getting to the formal discipline stage? And if it does, will ensure that members have the knowledge and courage to make tough love decisions – to vote to exclude a member, even a close friend or family member?

Gospel culture mood music

Such a church will believe that the gospel includes ongoing,

---

15 See nine case studies in Leeman, *Church Discipline*, 89–122.

growing holiness. In every Christian, whole-of-life holiness is gradual but inevitable and in a healthy gospel culture, members have 'bought in' to an expectation of transformation and the demands of discipleship. Members are hungry to be godlier. Sin is believed to be sad and bad for you. Holiness is believed to be joyful and good for you. The posture of repentance and faith is the way we all walk to the new creation.

Church culture mood music

The members of such a church invest in getting to know each other, in building meaningful, joyful, spiritually deliberate relationships, and making those relationships the norm in church life. The church is expected to be made up of credibly regenerate people – the purity of the body is presupposed: purity in belief; purity in behaviour; purity of the Lord's Supper. Church membership means I have a job to do. My job is to guard the purity of the church, maintain the good name of Jesus and to help other members to make it home in good shape.

In this church, unity 'at all costs' is not the aim because not all unity is good. There is a unity of death – everyone is united in a graveyard! There can be a unity of fear – there is unity under totalitarian regimes. There can be a unity of error. This church understands that disunity can actually be more biblical than some forms of unity! What is needed is a unity in truth.

Love culture mood music

We need churches where love reigns; love that laughs (with each other, not at each other); love that overlooks and bears with each other (Eph. 4:2); and love that speaks honest, humble words (Prov. 27:6). Love that warns, confronts, corrects. Love that raises the hand to remove your membership because you won't repent. Love that has your long-term end in heaven or hell in clear focus. Not a soppy, unconditional affirmation, an unprincipled, 'animal-like love'; but a God-like love that speaks the words that are hard to speak, and causes short-term pain for long-term gain.

Conclusion

Did you enjoy the chapter? I'm not sure you should enjoy a chapter on church discipline. If you did, perhaps you need to see your pastor! Because church discipline is always the result of sin, no one should enjoy this subject. Sin is sad. Sin is traumatic. And 'Love does not delight in evil' (1 Cor. 13:6). Church discipline in its formal sense is messy and complicated. It is agonising and exhausting. Church discipline is potentially, and often, divisive. (If you are not ready to be labelled unloving and divisive in even the clearest cases of church discipline, you're not ready.)

Yet when churches love Christ enough to take this seriously, Christ smiles. We desperately need to be members of a church where we'll not be comforted in our sin, but confronted about our sin.

Take courage. Trust God. Don't do it (unless it's absolutely necessary) until you've taught your people. Prepare prospective members that the church will love them enough to say hard things for their good. Prepare prospective members that this will be one of their jobs in the church. This is why being a committed member of a gospel church is the safest place to be.

Church discipline rightly used is (by God's grace) the love that rescues,[16] the love that heals,[17] the love that purifies, the love that shows that we really do love the offender, the other members, the world and the Lord Jesus.

P.S. Great news! D repented completely and C Baptist Church forgave him, brought him back into membership and received him at the Lord's Table. You can probably read his story in 1 Corinthians 5 and 2 Corinthians 2:5-11.

Questions for discussion

1. How should we define church discipline?
2. Why do local churches often neglect this practice today?
3. Talk about the surprising ways that love and church discipline connect. What goes wrong if a church practises discipline without love or shows love but never disciplines?
4. Read Matthew 18:15-19, 1 Corinthians 5:1-13 and

---

16 Eric Bargerhuff, *The Love that Rescues* (Wipf & Stock, 2010).

17 John White and Ken Blue, *Church Discipline That Heals* (IVP, 1992).

2 Corinthians 2:5-11. When should a healthy church discipline one of its members? How should they do it?

5. Reflect on these questions:

   i.   Are there hyper-individualist or consumerist attitudes in me when it comes to church?

   ii. Am I showing my responsibility for the church family and accepting their responsibility for me?

   iii. Am I willing to have my sin gently corrected by my loving gospel church family and to help do the same for others?

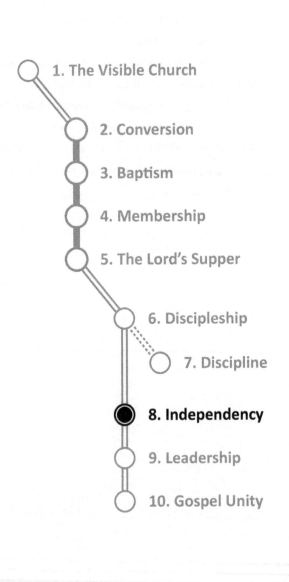

1. The Visible Church

2. Conversion

3. Baptism

4. Membership

5. The Lord's Supper

6. Discipleship

7. Discipline

8. Independency

9. Leadership

10. Gospel Unity

8. Independency

The local basis for making decisions together
Mike Gilbart-Smith

8. *We believe that each local church has final authority to admit and dismiss members, appoint and remove leaders, and establish the doctrinal and moral standards of the church. These processes should be implemented at regular church members' meetings.*

The last ten years had been quite extraordinary. Chichester Cross Community Church (C⁴ for short) had been started with just a dozen adults from another local church. It had been popular with new families moving into the area, and had seen a number of conversions. The church had grown to 200 adults on a Sunday morning and was bursting at the seams in the primary school that they had been renting.

This is when the trouble started. The pastor (the only church employee) had discovered that there was a local Working Men's club that was on the market. It had a hall and other rooms that were perfect for the needs of the church. He shared his vision with the church. A fund was started, and soon he declared that there was enough to get a deposit on the building, and that a mortgage would not be much more than the rent for the school building. Though some were unhappy at the church getting into debt, and others felt that it was taking up too much of the pastor's time, the congregation was happy that the Lord seemed to be providing for the church's future needs.

However, when an accountant in the church offered his help with the project finances, the pastor politely declined, then became quite defensive. With his wife and another close friend in the church, the accountant confronted the pastor. Eventually he confessed that he had borrowed several thousand pounds from the building fund without letting anyone know. His own finances were in trouble and he had been confident that he could pay it all back within a few months, but now he needed more time.

The three friends were shocked and saddened, but at a loss as to what to do. Having met and prayed together, they went to speak to the pastor again, and told him they thought that he must step down for behaving immorally and illegally. 'But the church will never recover,' retorted the pastor. 'Look, how about you lend me the money, I can then pay the church back immediately and nobody in the congregation need know.' They were horrified and pleaded with him, but he refused to step down.

The three again went and conferred. The pastor seemed to treat his sin so lightly. What should they do now? Major decisions had always been made by the pastor, and honestly they had genuinely trusted him.

One of them suggested holding a meeting of all who came to the church. But that included non-Christians, and it didn't seem right that such a significant spiritual decision as removing a pastor from office should be entrusted to such a mixed group. Another suggested they speak to the leaders of the church that originally sent out this church-plant. The third suggested getting advice from the national fellowship of churches to which the church belonged. Soon they were speaking to an employment lawyer within the fellowship of churches who examined the trust deed of the church. The trustees were four of the twelve founding members of the church. One was the pastor, two had moved away, and the fourth was the pastor's closest friend. The trust deed was clear that the pastor could only be removed from office if a majority of the three other trustees voted to remove him.

They requested a meeting with the trustees, who seemed to listen carefully to their concerns, but said that they must have a confidential conversation with the pastor, and would let them know their decision.

A week later the trustees wrote to them saying that they had considered the matter carefully, and following the model of Jesus himself, had paid the pastor's debt, and that was the end of the matter. They also warned the three not to tell anyone else in the church, as it might undermine the great work that the Lord had done over the last ten years. The three friends felt devastated, but powerless.

Did it matter?

Ability and responsibility

Of course, C⁴ is a fictional church. But, in such situations, who should have made the call as to whether the pastor was disqualified from ministry by his actions? Does the Bible give any indication as to who should make such decisions? Are there any commands in the Bible to take responsibility? And if so, had the trust deed of C⁴ given those people the *ability* to fulfil that *responsibility*? Were the three friends right to think that not only the wrong decision had been taken, but the wrong people had taken it?

The question addressed in this chapter is: to whom are these responsibilities given? Can an individual church, or group of churches, or a secular government or a nation decide who has what responsibilities within the church, or does the Bible itself delineate those responsibilities? The answers to such questions were assumed for hundreds of years: authority, and therefore responsibility, lay within the structures of the Roman Catholic Church. There were priests, bishops, cardinals and supremely the Pope, who were the guardians of the church. However, when in the Reformation the supreme authority of the church was challenged by the cry *Sola Scriptura*, the question of where authority within the church lay became once again an open question.

In the generation after the Reformation, different groups of Christians reached different conclusions as to where the *final* human responsibility for the membership, doctrine and morality of the church lay. Episcopalians argued that the church was to be overseen by bishops (the word used to translate the Greek word *episcopos*, literally 'overseer', in some Bible translations). The bishops themselves were to be answerable to the secular authority (particularly the monarch) in an established national church. Presbyterians argued that the office of elder (*presbuteros*) and overseer (*episcopos*) were one and the same, and that the church was to be overseen by teaching elders who would gather from several local churches in presbyteries, and they themselves would meet with other presbyteries from other areas in synods to make decisions for the wider church in a nation, and hypothetically across the whole world. Essential to Presbyterianism is the idea that 'many particular congregations may be under one church government.'[1] Independents agreed with Presbyterians on the unity of the offices of elder and bishop, but argued that elders were responsible only for the local church, and there were to be no presbyteries or synods with authority over local congregations. Like other Independents, Congregationalists argued for the independence of the local church, but added that within local churches, the elders themselves were answerable to the whole membership of the congregation, who were the final human authority in membership.

Does it matter? Is the Bible clear? Are the descriptions of how the church was governed in the New Testament merely descriptive of a moment in history, or should they be taken as prescriptive for all churches? One thing is clear: there was

---

1 'The Form of Presbyterial Church Government: 1645', in Iain Murray (ed.), *The Reformation of the Church* (The Banner of Truth Trust 1965), 219.

no universal church order within all churches. We can see this due to the fact that elders were not initially appointed in every town as churches were planted. Churches existed quite legitimately *without* elders, at least temporarily.[2] Therefore, any biblical church order that is to be argued for is not *essential* to the existence of a church, though highly beneficial for its maturity. Rather, I shall argue in this chapter, that congregationalism is in fact *more* fundamental to the government of the local church than even the existence of elders in each church. Under the Holy Spirit the church is both competent and responsible to discern what a Christian is (through her understanding of the gospel) and who should be treated as a Christian (through the preservation and maintenance of a true doctrine and morality within the church). These responsibilities are given to the local church *as a whole* and may not be passed onto a smaller group within the church or those outside of the congregation.

What are the responsibilities Jesus has given to the whole church?

Many of the responsibilities given to the church become particularly clear in the negative, and the positive becomes clearer by implication. For example, we shall see that the church has the final authority in putting people *out* of church membership through church discipline. An implication of this will be that the church also must have final responsibility

---

2 See Titus 1:5; Acts 14:21-23.

for *admitting* people into church membership. The church has the responsibility to remove *false* teachers and elders. Therefore the church must have responsibility in recognising faithful elders. The church has the responsibility to silence false teaching within the church. Therefore the church must have the responsibility to recognise the true preaching of the gospel.

Like cashiers in the bank who must recognise and reject the forged banknotes, by implication they also have the responsibility of recognising and accepting the genuine currency.

Who belongs?   1. Discipline

A key responsibility given to the church is the question of who belongs to the church. Jesus does not talk frequently about the church in the Gospels. The only two verses in which Jesus uses the word 'church' (Greek *ekklēsia*) are in Matthew's Gospel, where Jesus is talking about *what* a Christian is and *who* is a Christian. In Matthew 18, Jesus tasks the church to remove from the visible covenant people of God the unrepentant sinner:

> If your brother sins against you, go and tell him his fault, between you and him alone. If he listens to you, you have gained your brother. But if he does not listen, take one or two others along with you, that every charge may be established by the evidence of two or three witnesses. If he refuses to listen to them, tell it to the church. And if he refuses to listen even to the church,

> let him be to you as a Gentile and a tax collector. Truly, I say to you, whatever you bind on earth shall be bound in heaven, and whatever you loose on earth shall be loosed in heaven. Again I say to you, if two of you agree on earth about anything they ask, it will be done for them by my Father in heaven. For where two or three are gathered in my name, there am I among them. (Matt. 18:15-20)[3]

The 'brother's' (or sister's) unrepentant sin has called into question his (or her) profession of faith, and so the whole church is to take two steps in calling them to repentance. After two or three have failed to persuade them to repent, the whole church is to speak to the errant party. If they do not listen to the church speaking with one voice, the church herself is to treat them as a Gentile or tax collector, that is, one who is not a member of the covenant community of the church. Jesus doesn't say 'Tell it to the elders', 'Tell it to the bishop', or 'Tell it to the pastor', but 'Tell it to the church.' In the previous stages of taking one or two others along, it might be very wise for that to be one or two of the elders of the church, but Jesus himself insists that the church herself must speak with one voice to the errant brother or sister, and that only the church may ultimately take the step of removing them from visible covenant membership.

The apostle Paul recognises the need for the whole church's involvement in church discipline. Remarkably he sees even his own apostolic authority as insufficient for the removal of even the most obviously errant professing Christian from the

---

3 Scripture quotations in this chapter are ESV.

membership of the Corinthian church.

> For though absent in body, I am present in spirit; and as if present, I have already pronounced judgment on the one who did such a thing. When you are assembled in the name of the Lord Jesus and my spirit is present, with the power of our Lord Jesus, you are to deliver this man to Satan for the destruction of the flesh, so that his spirit may be saved in the day of the Lord. (1 Cor. 5:3-5)

Only the whole gathered Corinthian congregation was finally able to 'deliver this man to Satan' – that is to say, they were no longer to be considered part of the church comprised of those who were 'sanctified in Christ Jesus', 'called to be saints' and who were recipients of 'the grace of God that was given you in Christ Jesus' as those in 'the fellowship of his Son, Jesus Christ our Lord' (1 Cor. 1:2, 4, 9). Rather they were to be considered as those in the world, over which Satan rules. The apostle Paul, even as an apostle, could not bypass the local church, or just tell them what they must do in his name. Instead, he addresses them as the ones who must take responsibility, those who hold the keys of the kingdom for that member of the Corinthian church.

Who belongs? 2. Membership

Not only is this responsibility seen in the removal of people who are no longer showing evidence of being Christian, but also in the original inclusion within the church of those who are giving evidence of being disciples. We read earlier in Matthew 18 that Jesus delegates the responsibility that he has in heaven to the church on earth, to bind and loose. What does this look like on earth? The Great Commission fleshes out the responsibilities that the church is given to make disciples through the preaching of the gospel, and to recognise those disciples through believer's baptism (Matt. 28:18-20). Thus those who are to be baptised into Christ, and thereby into the church, are to be recognised as disciples by those who have the delegated authority of Christ on earth, namely the church. This makes sense when held together with the responsibility to discipline. It would be strange if a different group of people had the responsibility to remove from membership than those who have the responsibility of admitting to membership.[4] Ultimate responsibility for admitting to membership lies in the same place as responsibility to remove from membership. Those whom Christ gives the responsibility to bind, he also gives the responsibility to loose.[5]

---

4 To show the absurdity of having different people with the responsibilities of granting membership and exercising discipline, imagine that the elders had the responsibility to admit into membership, whereas the congregation had the responsibility to remove erring church members. This could lead to the highly divisive and undermining situation where the elders think that someone should be admitted whom the congregation thinks should be excluded. This person could be repeatedly admitted by the elders and then excluded by the congregation until one of them gave up on their responsibility!

5 For an excellent treatment of Jesus' meaning in Matthew 18 see chapter 4 'The Covenant of Love' in Leeman's, *The Church and the Surprising Offense of God's Love*, 229-270.

What is taught? 1. Silencing false gospels

Once we have seen Jesus delegating responsibility to the congregation in the recognition of the true believers in the gospel, it comes as no surprise that the church herself is given a second responsibility to preserve and protect the preaching of the true gospel. Those who are to baptise true believers are also to teach true doctrine. This is particularly clear when it comes to the central doctrine of the gospel itself.

The Galatian churches were being torn apart as people were 'quickly deserting him who called you in the grace of Christ and are turning to a different gospel – not that there is another one' (Gal. 1:6-7). This is the most urgent situation addressed in all of Paul's letters, and tellingly, in this drastic situation he doesn't write to the bishop of Galatia, the senior pastors of the Galatian churches, or even their elders. He writes instead 'To the churches of Galatia' (1:2). Was this because these were the most theologically discerning of all Christians in the first century? No! They are those with whom Paul is 'astonished' and 'in the anguish of childbirth' and 'perplexed' about, because they are 'deserting' Jesus, and have become 'foolish' and 'bewitched' (1:6, 4:19, 4:20, 3:1). So uncertain is he of how they will even respond to this desperate letter that he admits 'I am afraid I may have laboured over you in vain' (4:11). Yet, it is to these churches on the brink of apostasy he writes. What is more, he entreats these churches that, when it comes to the rejecting of false gospels within their churches, they have a higher authority than even he or an angel of God.

> But even if we or an angel from heaven should preach to you a gospel contrary to the one we preached to you, let him be accursed. As we have said before, so now I say again: If anyone is preaching to you a gospel contrary to the one you received, let him be accursed. (Gal. 1:8-9)

Why would Paul say that these foolish Galatians have the competence to declare as cursed even an apostle with a false gospel? Are they more competent in recognising the gospel than Paul himself? Clearly not! Rather, they are responsible. He writes to them because the buck stops with them. Why? Because Jesus gave the responsibility to make disciples to the churches. As churches, they were bodies of people who had received the true gospel, and so were competent to recognise a false gospel 'contrary to the one received'. As Christian churches, they had received the Holy Spirit with the reception of the gospel. They had received the gospel of justification by faith, and were therefore competent to hold on to that gospel.

> Let me ask you only this: Did you receive the Spirit by works of the law or by hearing with faith? Are you so foolish? Having begun by the Spirit, are you now being perfected by the flesh? Did you suffer so many things in vain – if indeed it was in vain? Does he who supplies the Spirit to you and works miracles among you do so by works of the law, or by hearing with faith?' (Gal. 3:3-5)

What is taught?   2. Authorising the true preaching of the word

We saw earlier that the removal of apparently false believers through church discipline and the admitting of apparently true believers must lie with the same people. Likewise, the establishing of the appropriate doctrinal standards of the church must fall to the same body as those who are to declare false gospels accursed. How can false gospels be recognised except by seeing that they diverge from the true gospel? Again, once one sees the logical necessity of such a responsibility, one further sees how this ties in with the church's Great Commission responsibility positively 'to teach everything that [Jesus has] commanded' (Matt. 28:20). As Jim Sayers and Jon Stobbs have already argued in earlier chapters, doctrinal and moral clarity on the essential teachings of the Lord Jesus are well served by the congregation, under the leadership of their elders, agreeing to doctrinal standards in a statement of faith, and moral standards in a church covenant.

Who leads?   1. Removal

If the church has corporate responsibility for the recognition of true believers and the teaching of true doctrine, it is unsurprising that the church would also have a third responsibility for recognising those with teaching authority within the church.

The polity of a local church seems highly insignificant so long as everything is going well. In the happy times that we are enjoying in the local church I have served for the past several years, almost everything that the elders bring to church members' meetings tends to be agreed unanimously by the church. Some newer members might even be tempted to ask what is the point of the congregation voting on the admission or discipline of members, the election of officers, the annual church budget and other important matters in the direction of the church. Are the congregation merely rubber stamping the elders' proposals? Such a happy unity makes us look very like a church where the congregation has no such responsibilities. The same decisions would have been made had they been the sole responsibility of the elders. However, it is when elders start leading *badly* that the differences in church government become painfully evident. Particularly when those with that responsibility become false shepherds, wolves among the sheep, who has the *ability* to protect the sheep from the wolves?

If the elders stop preaching the gospel, who can remove them? The Bible seems to be clear that there is to be a mechanism for the rebuke and removal of elders who are not preaching or living the gospel.

> Do not admit a charge against an elder except on the evidence of two or three witnesses. As for those who persist in sin, rebuke them in the presence of all, so that the rest may stand in fear. In the presence of God and of Christ Jesus and of the elect angels I charge you to keep these rules without prejudging, doing nothing from partiality. (1 Tim. 5:19-21)

Such a process means that elders are protected from a personal grudge from one church member, but, like all other church members, are not above the discipline of the whole congregation, but subject to public discipline on the testimony of two or three witnesses. Such a process is entirely necessary if the congregation is able to fulfil its responsibility to silence false teaching as outlined above. Similarly, if an elder ceases to be qualified morally or in their ability to teach God's word, the congregation must be able to remove him, for the sake of the preservation of the teaching and living of the gospel in the whole congregation.

In one sense, in most situations in the world, every church is ultimately congregational. If there is no mechanism to vote a false teacher out of the pulpit, members of the congregation may vote with their feet, and join another church where the gospel is preached. However, this has the heart-breaking implication that the *faithful* have to jump ship while the faithless stay and shipwreck the church along with any who remain on board through confusion or weakness.

Who leads?   2. Approval

Once again, if the congregation has the responsibility to remove erring elders, it must follow that the congregation should have the final say in the recognition of new elders. In the New Testament there is only a little evidence for the mechanism of the appointment of elders. The Greek word used for appointment of elders is *cheirotoneō* (Acts 14:23, Titus 1:5). Etymologically this would imply voting (literally 'extending the hand'), though it is possible that some other form of appointment divorced from the word's literal etymology might be implied. By contrast, when Jesus appoints apostles, the more clearly unilateral terms *eklegō* (choose) and *poieō* (make) are used (Luke 6:13; Mark 3:14-15).

More explicitly, in Acts 6, with the appointment of the first deacons, despite the presence of the authoritative apostles, it is the 'full number of the disciples' whom the apostles exhort to 'pick out from among you seven men of good repute, full of the Spirit and of wisdom, whom we will appoint to this duty' (Acts 6:2-3). The authority of the apostles is recognised as they commission the deacons. The responsibility of the congregation is recognised as they pick them out.

How should congregational responsibilities be exercised?

There is little biblical material about how congregations should exercise the responsibilities that they have together. However, though the material is minimal, it is clear.

Jesus himself says, in the context of the congregational responsibility of church discipline, 'For where two or three are gathered in my name, there am I among them' (Matt. 18:20).

Paul follows the pattern of Jesus' teaching: 'When you are assembled in the name of the Lord Jesus and my spirit is present, with the power of our Lord Jesus, you are to deliver this man to Satan for the destruction of the flesh, so that his spirit may be saved in the day of the Lord (1 Cor. 5:4-5). Thus, it is clear that the corporate decisions of the church are to be taken when the whole church is gathered together in person. As we are present with one another, Christ is present with us leading us to declare on earth the will that he has in heaven.

This doesn't mean that congregations are incapable of making bad, or even godless decisions. Rather that, in accordance with everything Jesus has commanded us, and in dependence upon his Spirit, we are to declare and enact his will within his church.

Practically speaking this means that it is important to have scheduled members' meetings when the whole congregation might gather, without the visitors who might be present at public services of the church. Though there is nothing in the Bible saying how frequent these meetings should be, they should be regular enough that it will be easy for as many of the church as possible to gather.

Objections to the independency of the local church

What about elders' authority?

There are certainly responsibilities given to the elders of local churches. Those responsibilities come with a great weight. ('If anyone does not know how to manage his own family, how can he take care of God's church?' (1 Tim. 3:5)) The congregation is also given responsibility to submit to the leadership (presumably of elders) within the church. Though there is clear responsibility given to the elders of the church, this by no means contradicts the authority of the congregation herself, any more than the authority of Christ himself negates the authority that he himself gives to the elders and the congregation.

The 1648 Cambridge Platform drawn up by New England Congregationalists put it like this:

> The government of the church is a mixed government (and so hath been acknowledged long before the term independency was heard of). In respect of Christ, the head and king of the church, and the sovereign power residing in him, and exercised by him, it is a monarchy. In respect of the body, or brotherhood of the church, and power from Christ granted unto them, it resembles a democracy. In respect of the presbytery and power committed to them, it is an aristocracy.[6]

To say that elders have authority and therefore the congregation has none is to say that the police have authority and therefore the courts have none, or the courts have authority and therefore Parliament has none. The question is not *whether* each group has authority, but *what* their authority is, and therefore how the different authorities fit together. In various arenas outside the church we also see how different authorities can coexist so long as the bounds of authority are well understood. We recognise that limited and mutually accountable authorities are wise in this fallen world.

Similarly, in the secular authorities the police have the authority to arrest and to charge, but no authority to convict. The courts have authority to apply the law, and convict a

---

6 'The Cambridge Platform 1648', Murray (ed.), *The Reformation of the Church*, 255.

criminal, but Parliament may change the law. Parliament herself is answerable to the electorate.

Within the church, the elders certainly have a responsibility to teach God's word, but the church has the responsibility to silence an elder who preaches another gospel. The elders have the responsibility to lead an exemplary life, but the congregation has a responsibility to bring witnesses against an elder whose life denies the gospel. The elders have authority to counsel but their ultimate authority is the word of God. The command is in Scripture. Elders cannot command what Scripture does not.

What about Timothy and Titus?

We cannot argue from Scripture that there was one universal form of church government that was applied in every circumstance. For example, it is clear that Titus has teaching responsibility in multiple churches in Crete (Titus 1).[7] It is certainly clear that Titus exercises a much wider teaching authority than one local church. However, two things should be noted.

Firstly, just as an apostle or an angel could not override the Galatian churches' responsibility to preserve the gospel in their churches (Gal. 1:8), so also Titus' authority could

---

7 There was not a plurality of elders in every town. By analogy it is suggested that Timothy may have had similar authority in several congregations in Ephesus. Because the status of Timothy outside of the Ephesian church is less clear from the text, I will focus on Titus.

not trump congregational responsibility within the Cretan churches. His call to 'teach what accords with sound doctrine' (Titus 2:1) by no means gives him the personal authority to trump all other teaching authority within the church. On the contrary, he is to nurture churches in which members of the congregation will learn to teach one another. For Titus is to 'appoint elders in every town' who 'must hold firm to the trustworthy word as taught, so that [they] may be able to give instruction in sound doctrine and also to rebuke those who contradict it' (1:5, 9) and he must also ensure that there are older women who 'teach what is good, and so train the young women to love their husbands and children' (2:3-4).

Secondly, the supra-congregational teaching authority of a Titus was never intended to be a permanent solution, but it was a necessary interim measure. Since an elder 'must not be a recent convert' (1 Tim. 3:6), it was impossible to 'appoint elders in every town' until there were mature Christians in the Cretan churches who would qualify as elders. The appointment of such plural local leadership wasn't seen as an optional goal, but an essential step in the right ordering of the churches. More than that, the primary goal of Paul leaving Titus in a bishop-like role was to do himself out of a job by appointing local elders. 'This is why I left you in Crete, so that you might put what remained into order, and appoint elders in every town as I directed you' (1:5).

What about the council of Jerusalem?

Some see Acts 15, if not as a blueprint for the church, certainly as evidence that connectional authority above the local church is both permissible and desirable for the church of all ages. Acts 15:1-2 shows the backdrop to the situation:

> But some men came down from Judea and were teaching the brothers, 'Unless you are circumcised according to the custom of Moses, you cannot be saved.' And after Paul and Barnabas had no small dissension and debate with them, Paul and Barnabas and some of the others were appointed to go up to Jerusalem to the apostles and the elders about this question.

So after some conversation and debate with Pharisees in the Jerusalem church, 'the apostles and the elders, with the whole church' came to an agreement that there was no need for Gentile Christians to be circumcised, but agreed to send a letter affirming their freedom from circumcision and exhorting them 'that you abstain from what has been sacrificed to idols, and from blood, and from what has been strangled, and from sexual immorality' (15:22, 29). Whether or not this demonstrates the authority of the council [8] or merely the agreement of the Jerusalem church with what the apostle Paul had already been teaching, there are no sound arguments to see this as a precedent for extra-congregational authority. The circumstances of Acts 15 are not repeated in today's church. There are no apostles. There is a completed New Testament that is sufficient to settle all matters of dispute

---

8 It is not called a council in the text.

within a congregation. We have already seen that the Lord Jesus gives authority to preserve the gospel to the churches: even on exactly this issue of circumcision it was the churches of Galatia that were to refute a false gospel.[9]

What about the authority of the state?

In the providence of God, the authority of the British monarch over the Church of England in the sixteenth century was used for great good for the advancement of the gospel. Henry VIII's desire for an annulment of his marriage to Catherine of Aragon gave opportunity for the Reformation in England to advance, largely against the will of most of the clergy in the country. Regal authority under Edward VI enabled the Reformation to accelerate through the Acts of Uniformity of 1549 and 1552.

However, very thankfully for the history of the church, God's ability to use an illegitimately established human authority for his ends by no means legitimises that authority. It merely vindicates God's ultimate sovereignty. It is true that Christians are called to be faithful citizens, both praying for and submitting to secular authorities in this world. However, there is no New Testament call for the church to look to the secular authorities for spiritual leadership. More than that,

---

9 If, as is likely, Galatians is written before the events of Acts 15, it would be another argument against a council of Jerusalem settling the New Testament teaching on circumcision, as Paul is pretty clear that the gospel is very clear on this without the need to appeal to the council.

the testimony of history is that, more often than not, the state assuming authority over the church at best undermines the church's purity (as in the reign of Elizabeth I and almost every monarch since) and at worst persecutes those who are attempting to be most faithful to God's word.

An established national church may give some opportunities for the church to preach the gospel into the world, but far more often it gives opportunity for the world to infect the church.

Should we really divide on a secondary matter?

As the post-Reformation debates over the government of the church continued into the second half of the sixteenth century, the argument that effectively settled the debate within the Church of England was that of Richard Hooker's *Laws of Ecclesiastical Polity*. There Hooker argues that though *some* polity is necessary lest there be anarchy in the church, the manner of that polity need not be the same throughout the world, just as 'he which affirmeth speech to be necessary amongst all men throughout the world, doth not thereby import that all men must necessarily speak one kind of language.'[10] He continues that even if God himself gave a form of church polity, because it is not a salvation issue, it may have been appropriate only for the church at the time, and there may be better ways to reach the same ends of that polity:

10 Richard Hooker, *Laws of Ecclesiastical Polity*, Book 3, 352.

> I therefore conclude that neither God's being author of laws for government of his Church, nor his committing them unto Scripture, is any reason sufficient wherefore all churches should for ever be bound to keep them without change.[11]

How the church since Hooker has been plagued with the idea that only in that which is essential to salvation should we assume that God's word is authoritative and normative! While it is without doubt that primary gospel issues are of greater importance than secondary issues, that does not mean that secondary issues are of no importance. As we have seen above, the Lord Jesus has not merely given a gospel. He has given the church a Great Commission whereby he, in his kingly authority, has laid down how that gospel is to be preached to all nations, and how the church has the responsibility not only to preach it, but also to baptise, to disciple and to discipline. We must be obedient not only in obeying the gospel, but also in obeying *everything* that the Lord Jesus has commanded.

Conclusion: an outpost of heaven on earth

Local churches may fail. They may fail in their responsibility to preserve gospel preaching and living, and face the judgment of the Christ whose will they are called to enact. Many churches have had their lampstand removed and have become merely godless religious clubs, or have disappeared altogether. Others, through their very faithfulness, have attracted the wrath of a world that hates Jesus, and have been snuffed out

---

11 Hooker, *Laws of Ecclesiastical Polity*, 390.

by the one who loves to devour God's people. But each church is called to be a picture of a church that will never fail and can never be destroyed. Jesus has promised that the gates of hell will not prevail against it. His church will be a bride clothed in white, pure and radiant in her faithfulness. It will be a vast city walled into the brilliant presence of Christ in its security and joy.

Christ is building his church. He builds her by being present with her, and by calling her to faithfulness as she makes disciples of all nations, baptising and teaching them, and calling them to belong to him, even as he promises to be with them always, till the very end of the age.

Questions for Discussion

1. 'The polity [government] of a local church seems highly insignificant so long as everything is going well.' Who has the authority in your church to remove your teaching pastor if he should fall away theologically or morally?

2. In the generation after the Reformation what different conclusions did Christians reach on where final human responsibility for the church lay? Which one is argued for in this chapter?

3. What important gospel decisions are the whole membership of a local church responsible for? How does the congregation do this in your church?

4. What objections do some raise to the independency of the local church? How can they be answered?

5. Do you belong to an independent and congregationally governed church? If yes, then how can you ensure that you take your responsibilities seriously going forward? If no, then do you know who takes these decisions and why? If you are not sure, then who can you ask?

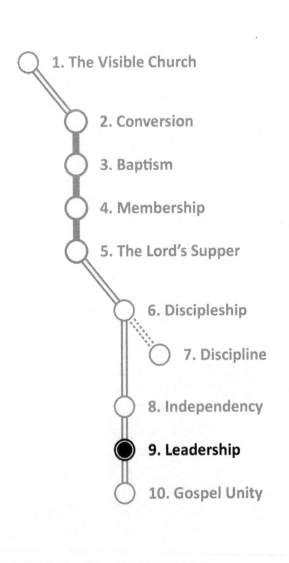

1. The Visible Church
2. Conversion
3. Baptism
4. Membership
5. The Lord's Supper
6. Discipleship
7. Discipline
8. Independency
9. Leadership
10. Gospel Unity

9. Leadership

The local people given to teach and guide

Brad Franklin

9. *We believe that each local church should be led, taught, and prayed over by a plurality of godly and suitably gifted elders, as defined in the Pastoral Epistles, and served by similarly godly deacons, who, for the sake of unity, and for the upholding of the ministry of the word, are to care for particular needs arising in the life of the church.*

Leadership matters

Leadership is always in the news – whether it's contentious elections, dictatorial regimes, or just further haggling over Britain's role in Europe. The discussion on a national and global scale is hard to avoid. Maybe your concerns only extend so far as your local council or the new head at your daughter's school, but the fact remains: you (and nearly everybody else) have an opinion about who's in charge. Leadership matters. It matters who makes the decisions, who makes the rules, who spends our money (and how they spend it).

It matters who steers the moral agenda and geopolitically who has their 'finger on the button'! If leadership matters in the world of politics, corporations, hospitals, sewing clubs and schools, how much more should it matter in the local church – the body that is 'God's household, which is the church of the living God, the pillar and foundation of the truth' (1 Tim. 3:15).[1]

This chapter will argue that the local church should be led, taught and prayed for by a plurality of godly and gifted men serving as elders. Simultaneously, the local church should be served by godly deacons who promote unity in the body and uphold the ministry of the word by facilitating practical ministry in the life of the church. Scripture gives us this pattern. Both offices, when filled by qualified individuals, help the church fulfil her commission. As this book has collectively argued, a *pure* bride of Christ is better equipped to proclaim the gospel and adorn that gospel by her life together.

Sadly, the church at large is confused on leadership. Ask your unbelieving neighbour: 'Who runs the church?' and you'd get a blank stare (at best) or some vague answer about a priest (at worst). This is expected in twenty-first-century Britain. Here's the difficult bit: would you get a better answer from most of your church? Maybe they'd substitute 'minister' for 'priest'?

---

1 Scripture quotations in this chapter are NIV.

Work needs doing

We need to reconsider the Bible's teaching on leadership. Maybe you hear the word 'deacon', and your eyes glaze over? These topics aren't 'page-turners' for most! Or maybe you just feel awkward talking about leadership? You've been burned by an abusive leader in the past, or thinking about this may lead to difficult conversations in your church right now. This discomfort with authority (let alone our apathy about it) is enough to keep even the bravest souls from talking about leadership. We have to ask ourselves: is it *possible* to have godly leaders in the church who wield authority well? By virtue of the fact that God gives us qualifications for such leaders (1 Tim. 3; Titus 1) we must answer 'yes'. Would it be beneficial for us to have leaders like this? Of course it would be!

Well then, whether we find the topic boring or difficult, work needs doing in every church. We must go back to the Bible, so that we might recognise and appoint leaders who will govern well. We need leaders like those David alluded to from his death bed: 'When one rules over people in righteousness, when he rules in the fear of God, he is like the light of morning at sunrise on a cloudless morning, like the brightness after rain that brings grass from the earth' (2 Sam. 23:3b-4). What blessing this kind of leadership would bring to your church and mine! Let's get to work by rethinking what the Bible teaches on elders.

Elders

What do we call our leaders?

Names and titles are important. Ask any new parent labouring to get just the right name as their nine months of pregnancy draws to an end! Sophia? Sammy? Susan? Ahhh! Or ask the person recently named CEO of some big city firm or the newly appointed assistant manager of your local supermarket. Titles matter, because they communicate significant realities and sometimes responsibilities. The primary name or title Scripture gives to church leaders is 'elder'. Look at Acts 20. There, Paul is wrapping up his last recorded missionary journey, and he knows that he will be arrested in Jerusalem. While passing near Ephesus, he calls a meeting with the 'elders' (v. 17) of the Ephesian church. He wants to impart his farewell and final instructions. Notice the titles Paul uses as he speaks to them: 'Keep watch over yourselves and all the flock of which the Holy Spirit has made you overseers. Be shepherds of the church of God, which he bought with his own blood' (Acts 20:28). Paul calls these elders 'overseers' or 'bishops'. Then, he tells them to 'be shepherds' or serve as pastors of God's church. In a few verses, three titles interchangeably refer to the same group of men. All three point to the same office, and all three will come up again in the New Testament referring to church leaders. Elders are overseers, *and* they're pastors. But why three names? Possibly because each name (though overlapping) hints at a different facet of church leadership. 'Elder' points to a spiritual maturity required for the office –

though a man may not necessarily be older in age. 'Overseer' denotes leadership and decision-making responsibilities. 'Pastor' makes clear the elder's responsibility to feed, nurture and protect God's flock like a shepherd does his sheep.

How many elders should there be?

How many elders should a church have? The biblical pattern is: more than one. Clearly, the church in Ephesus (Acts 20:17-28) had a plurality. That was also Paul's intention for the church on Crete. He instructed Titus: 'The reason I left you in Crete was that you might put in order what was left unfinished and appoint elders in every town, as I directed you' (Titus 1:5). The churches on Crete were *not* to have one pastor with some deacons to help him – but *elders*; elders (plural) in every town (singular) where a church had been planted on the island. Nowhere in Scripture do we find a church led by one man (cf. Acts 14:23, 21:18; James 5:14), despite the prevalence of this practice today.

There's a pattern across Scripture: some of the elders are set apart 'full time' for their work, and they're even paid for their labours as church finance allows (1 Tim. 5:18). Other elders have a 'day job' (maybe as a teacher, mechanic or project manager) and still serve as elders of God's flock. Though one elder may carry the majority of the teaching load (as his time is set apart to the task), all of the elders are equal in authority and responsibility. The benefits offered to a church in having multiple elders are many:

- Individual strengths and biblical wisdom are pooled and weaknesses neutralised;
- Leadership goes beyond one man, encouraging stability and continuity if one man fails morally, moves on or is called to glory;
- Accountability is promoted as a protection against abuse;
- The pastoral burden is shared and, ideally, this strengthens pastoral care.

Phil A. Newton strikes the balance:

> Here is precisely the wisdom of the New Testament pattern of plural eldership. No man possesses all the gifts necessary for leading a congregation. Some men are endowed with strong pulpit gifts, but lack pastoral skills. Others excel in pastoral work of visiting and counseling, but are not strong when it comes to pulpit exposition. Some have unusual abilities in organizing and administrating the ministries of the church, but fail in pulpit and counseling skills. Some, to be sure, are multi-gifted and capable of enormous work at different levels. But the strain of tending to the entire ministry needs of the church can quickly deplete even the most gifted men.[2]

Plural eldership is both biblical and wise for the church and for the elders themselves.

---

2 Phil A. Newton, *Elders in Congregational Life* (Kregel Publications, 2005), 38-39.

What do elders actually do?

The old joke goes that pastors have the easiest job in the world – they only work on Sundays! In reality of course, the elder's job is much, much more. The task of the elder could be summarised, again, by Acts 20:28: 'Keep watch over yourselves and all the flock of which the Holy Spirit has made you overseers. Be shepherds of the church of God, which he bought with his own blood'. For those who have grown up in urban or suburban environments, the illustration of a shepherd is partially lost. Actual shepherds have long hours, trying weather, and the difficulty of working with silly sheep! If you want to learn what elders are to do, go to your nearest pasture and watch! Peter makes the same point to elders: 'Be shepherds of God's flock that is under your care' (1 Pet. 5:2). Elders look to literal shepherds to understand their job, ultimately looking to the Good Shepherd (John 10:11, 15).

Like shepherds, elders must:

- Feed the sheep the word of God;
- Care for the hurting, weary and even straying sheep;
- Lead the flock (especially by exemplary lives – 1 Pet. 5:3) towards godliness and productivity;
- Protect the flock from false teaching and other dangers.

As churches look for men to serve as elders, they ought to look for shepherds. Who has genuine love and concern for the flock? Who is like Jesus – quietly setting an example by their life? Who is already 'shepherding' (even without the title)? The goal is healthy and productive sheep, and sheep need shepherds. God's provision is godly elders.

So, how specifically does an elder *actually* 'shepherd'? By two principal tasks: teaching and praying. Let's take each task in turn. Elders feed, lead and equip the sheep, firstly, by teaching the Bible – preaching, leading Bible studies, counselling, etc. Paul exhorts Timothy to 'Preach the word; be prepared in season and out of season; correct, rebuke and encourage – with great patience and careful instruction' (2 Tim. 4:2). Elders should teach the word of God – especially the good news about Jesus – in a variety of public and private settings. An elder must: 'hold firmly to the trustworthy message as it has been taught, so that he can encourage others by sound doctrine and refute those who oppose it' (Titus 1:9). Every elder may not preach publicly every Lord's Day, but every elder has a responsibility to handle the Bible well and help God's people with it. Part of teaching is also faithfully administering both baptism and the Lord's Supper to the gathered church – the two 'wordless' sermons Jesus has mandated. Through their teaching, the elders aim for Christlikeness (Col. 1:28-29) in God's people, and they labour to see a body equipped to carry out the church's disciple-making ministry (Matt. 28:19-20; Eph. 4:11-16). God builds his church by his word, therefore elders teach.

Elders also shepherd by praying. We will return to this shortly, but in Acts 6:3-4, the apostles set the pattern for the elders who would follow them. 'We ... will give our attention to prayer and the ministry of the word' (Acts 6:3-4). Notice, the apostles emphasise *prayer* and the ministry of the word. If the apostles themselves prioritised prayer in the formative days of the New Testament church, how much more ought the elders to pray today? Elders must plead with God for the spread of the gospel, bring before the Lord the needs of the church both locally and globally, and cry out for God's forgiveness, strength, wisdom and help. It's God who brings growth, so elders pray (1 Cor. 3:6-7) and lead the church to pray.

It is assumed that if elders are going to shepherd well, they know their sheep intimately. Teaching and praying will fall flat if not built on the foundation of close relationships. Elders must, as one writer puts it, 'smell like sheep!'[3] They need to know the flock's temptations, needs, gifts and passions. Therefore they need to be good listeners. There is no substitute for extended time together – through formal church meetings and more relaxed, personal time. Elders ought to open up their homes and their lives and even *enjoy* fun time with their church family. Often, for me, this happens over food! This may sound like madness to some, but how else could you expect to teach them and pray for them well? Sheep follow shepherds, if they know those shepherds love them. Richard Baxter speaks to elders about this:

> When the people see that you unfeignedly love them, they will hear anything and bear anything from you ... We ourselves will take all things well from one that we know doth entirely love us.

3   Jeramie Rinne, *Church Elders* (Crossway, 2014), 31.

> We will put up with a blow that tis given us in love, sooner than
> with a foul word that is spoken to us in malice or in anger.[4]

This kind of love takes time and united effort. It makes sense that a church's elders would regularly meet together to pray and plan how best to lead and care for the church. Practically, it would be very difficult for a group of elders to look after a church and never meet to discuss that care. Elders' meetings (whatever their frequency) should fuel shepherding – prayer and teaching.

In summary, elders shepherd – by teaching, praying, caring, serving and setting an example for the church. If done faithfully, this will take slightly more than one hour a week! Elders are not necessarily amazing orators, successful businessmen, visionary leaders, or self-help gurus. Elders are shepherds who love God and God's flock.

What kind of people must elders be?

Pick any industry, and you'll hear the same line: character matters. We all care that nurses are diligent, teachers are compassionate, bank executives are honest, lorry drivers aren't drunks, politicians don't love money, and film producers aren't sexual predators. We want bosses, colleagues and friends that are morally upright. In his wisdom, God has designed his church to be led by men of just such distinction. What is the principal requirement for a man to serve as

---

4 Richard Baxter, *The Reformed Pastor* (The Banner of Truth Trust, 1656, reprt. 2007), 118.

an elder? Godly character. 1 Timothy 3:1-7 and Titus 1:6-9 provide the qualifications one must meet to serve as an elder. If someone does not possess all of these qualities, he is not yet ready to serve as an elder.

In 1 Timothy, before Paul outlines this character, he makes one key distinction. The role of elder is open only to men. Two bits of evidence in 1 Timothy support this. In chapter two, Paul bars women from teaching or holding authority over men in the local church: 'A woman should learn in quietness and full submission. I do not permit a woman to teach or to assume authority over a man; she must be quiet' (1 Tim. 2:11-12). Then in chapter three, Paul explicitly describes the type of *men* that elders must be. This is categorically *not* denigrating to women, because it does tell us that men and women are different by God's good design. These ideas, of course, aren't unique to Paul. In fact, this pattern of male leadership is drawn right from the creation of man and woman in Genesis 1-2. The current cultural moment rails against these ideas, but what is at stake is the character of God and the authority of the Bible. Scripture is clear. Will we submit to it – admitting that God is good and knows better than us?

As 1 Timothy 3 proceeds, Paul lists fifteen qualities elders must possess.

> Here is a trustworthy saying: Whoever aspires to be an overseer desires a noble task. Now the overseer is to be above reproach, faithful to his wife, temperate, self-controlled, respectable, hospitable, able to teach, not given to drunkenness, not violent but gentle, not quarrelsome, not a lover of money. He must

> manage his own family well and see that his children obey him, and he must do so in a manner worthy of full respect. (If anyone does not know how to manage his own family, how can he take care of God's church?) He must not be a recent convert, or he may become conceited and fall under the same judgment as the devil. He must also have a good reputation with outsiders, so that he will not fall into disgrace and into the devil's trap. (1 Tim. 3:1-7)

The list is not exhaustive, and the qualifications are rather 'ordinary'. These are expectations (except being 'able to teach') that every Christian should aspire to. 'Above reproach' (v. 2) serves as a 'catch all' term. If a man's business dealings, home life, hobbies or personal behaviour in any way raise obvious red flags to his church family (or 'outsiders' – v. 7), he ought not to be an elder yet. That's why Paul says he must practise sexual fidelity, be self-controlled, use his home and life to serve others, not be enslaved to alcohol, not be a recent convert, etc. This is what it looks like to be 'above reproach'. The only two skills in this list are that a man must be 'able to teach' (which we discussed earlier) and 'manage his home well'. Ultimately, a man's home life is a testing ground for elder-preparedness. If a man's 'house' is chronically in chaos, he's not yet suitable to manage God's 'house'. If he has children, they must 'believe' (or better 'be trustworthy') which means they must not be 'open to the charge of being wild and disobedient' (Titus 1:6). Elders are not required to be married and have children, but elders are to be the type of men that provide leadership in their home (whoever might be in it).

It is better not to have elders than to have unqualified

men serving the church, thus Paul left this 'unfinished' in the Cretan churches (Titus 1:5). Yet this list of qualifications is what Jesus wants the men who lead his church to be like. As we consider this list, isn't it good? Don't we want bosses, parents, or politicians like this? Many are troubled by abuse scandals that have rocked various wings of 'Christianity' over the years (and rightly so!). Why do these abuses happen? For lots of reasons, obviously, but one reason rises to the top: unqualified men have been leading churches. This list of qualifications is a protection (not a guarantee, of course) against power-hungry, self-aggrandising men and equally it's a protection against weak, passive men. This list describes men who will wield authority humbly to benefit those under their care. Surely, all who read this will have known leaders who wielded authority well – coaches, teachers, parents or pastors. They were strong and active but gentle and loving, and we loved them for it! God used them to change us for good! Twenty-first-century Britain is a hard place to be a leader (especially a man in leadership). This list in 1 Timothy 3 shows what we're looking for, and it's good. We need biblically qualified elders leading our churches.

What should I do if our church *currently* doesn't have men like this (other than our pastor)? Firstly, pray for more elders. Ultimately, it is God who raises up shepherds for his sheep. Secondly though – prepare yourself, this is going to be 'ground-breaking' – train the men you *do* have! Paul urged Timothy: 'what you have heard from me in the presence of many witnesses entrust to faithful men, who will be able to

teach others also' (2 Tim. 2:2, ESV). What's stopping your
church from doing this? You don't need lots of money or
formal theological courses (although these certainly help).
Churches, under God, raise up elders. Maybe you could read
and discuss a good book on eldership with an older man in
your church? Or maybe give a young man the opportunity to
preach one evening (and then give him feedback)? If you are
currently a 'solo' pastor, model a loving shepherding ministry
for long enough, and, by example, you will be training men
to help carry the load. At the same time, pro-actively work
with the men God has given you.

Deacons

Relative to other big cities, London is a clean city. In my
better moments, I realise this about the city in which I live,
and I'm thankful for it. I'm especially thankful for those who
keep our borough clean – the bin men, the leaf-rakers, the
graffiti clean-up team, and those saints who keep the sewers
clear. So many, by their unseen work, make our city a better
place to live. Similarly, the church is made better by the
practical, often unseen service of many – especially deacons.
Deacons support the elders, unite the church and help meet
practical needs.

The problem

Acts 6:1-7 describes a problem every gospel-preaching church
wants to deal with. The number of disciples is growing! But

this leads to more needs, more potential disputes and more hurt feelings. 'In those days when the number of disciples was increasing, the Hellenistic Jews among them complained against the Hebraic Jews because their widows were being overlooked in the daily distribution of food' (Acts 6:1). The problem: in a majority Aramaic-speaking church, some of the minority, Greek-speaking widows were being forgotten. It was a logistics breakdown that led to complaining and (assumedly) disunity. The church's witness for Christ was under threat ('They're the church that says they love each other, but Gabriella and Hana have been hungry for days!'), and the apostles, if called upon to sort this, would have to neglect prayer and proclaiming the gospel. This situation, if left unresolved, would have been devastating. The issues and threats of the Acts 6 church are with us today. The church's unity, witness and disciple-making task can easily be 'derailed' by practical problems. This sounds rather twenty-first century, and differences in language or culture merely aggravate these issues. Practical problems do need practical solutions.

The solution

The practical solution the apostles offer to this practical problem is godly practical people. 'Brothers and sisters, choose seven men from among you who are known to be full of the Spirit and wisdom. We will turn this responsibility over to them and will give our attention to prayer and the ministry of the word' (Acts 6:3-4). They set responsible people over the food distribution and set them loose to make it happen and (presumably) bring others along to help. Many scholars recognise these men in Acts 6 as 'proto-deacons.' It is true, these seven are never called 'deacons'; but looking back at how the role is described, the Greek word for deacon is used twice to describe what they actually do. In verse 1, they 'daily distribute' food or 'deacon' food. In verse 2, the apostles say they must not neglect their ministry to 'deacon' tables. These men 'deacon' and thus set the pattern for the office later to be formalised in Paul's letters. Here in Acts 6, these men are described as 'full of the Holy Spirit' and 'wise.' 1 Timothy 3 provides a more extensive list of qualifications for those who fill the office of deacon:

> Deacons are to be worthy of respect, sincere, not indulging in much wine, and not pursuing dishonest gain. They must keep hold of the deep truths of the faith with a clear conscience. They must first be tested; and then if there is nothing against them, let them serve as deacons. In the same way, the women are to be worthy of respect, not malicious talkers but temperate and trustworthy in everything. A deacon must be faithful to his wife and must manage his children and his household well. Those who have served well gain an excellent standing and great assurance in their faith in Christ Jesus. (1 Tim. 3:8-13)

From my perspective, this text allows that deacons can be women as well as men, and the example of Phoebe the deacon in Romans 16:1 appears to confirm this. Yet because of 1 Timothy 2 and the biblical pattern of male headship in the church, it would be unwise for women to serve as deacons if the office was confused with that of elders (as often happens) or a position of authority in the church. Deacons are godly men or women who support the elders' ministry of the word and prayer (the work passed down from the apostles) and unite the church by meeting practical needs.

These deacons must be sensitive to the needs of the church and recognise that their particular task is actually a help to the whole. Thus, deacons must be peacemakers, encouragers and joyful servants who grasp that administration and service are a means to unity (e.g. Acts 6). Few things bog the elders down more than practical needs looming and nobody stepping up. If a roof leak doesn't get fixed, if rotas for coffee or childcare are not done, if the PA system is not quite right every week, if a redecoration project is looming, if widows aren't being looked after – the whole church suffers and the elders feel the pressure to sort these things themselves (potentially to the neglect of other responsibilities).

It is helpful to see deacons not necessarily as an office that someone holds for life, but as an individual appointed to meet a specific need (like the proto-deacons in Acts 6). Thus, the church could have (for example) a deacon for hospitality who organises coffee rotas and facilitates shared lunches, a deacon for mercy ministries who coordinates elderly care or assists those with financial needs, a deacon for the building who coordinates upkeep and repairs, a deacon for finance who maintains the church accounts, etc. Other deacon roles could be created as needed or wrapped up if no longer necessary, and thus, the deacons need not see themselves as another 'board' under the elders but a focused office adapting to and meeting your church's changing needs.

The result

In Acts 6, one can't help but notice the obvious results of the appointment of deacons. 'So the word of God spread. The number of disciples in Jerusalem increased rapidly, and a large number of priests became obedient to the faith' (Acts 6:7). The point is unavoidable: the church was unified, the apostles were freed up to minister the word and pray, and the church's all-round witness was strengthened. This happens, at least in part, because deacons are appointed. These seemingly small, unseen roles (like my local bin men!) make a world of difference.

Conclusion

Of course, how a church is run and who leads it isn't the gospel. You can hear again the persuasive voices: 'Should we not just proclaim Christ?' This sounds so right. The context of Acts 6 helps us in this wider conversation too. We could just talk about Jesus, but, notice, that's not what the apostles did! They knew (as all of the New Testament bears out) a well-ordered church both supports and adorns the gospel we proclaim. On this point, all the chapters of this book essentially hang together. As the gospel is faithfully proclaimed, the spiritually dead are raised to life. Then, these new believers join the covenant community of the local church through the waters of baptism. This local church family gathers regularly under the preached word and around the Lord's Supper. When necessary, unrepentant members are called to account (and ideally restored) through corrective church discipline. I could walk through each chapter! All of this protects and adorns the gospel, and an integral piece of the whole grand design is church leadership. It's obvious: you can't make disciples effectively (cf. Matt. 28:19-20) with a poorly led or divided church! Thankfully, as we have seen, God has given us the pattern we need in his word. As the local church is led by qualified elders, and as these elders are practically assisted by godly deacons, the church *will* be better equipped to make disciples as she is meant to. Leadership matters – in Scripture and in practice. Let's line our churches up with the pattern Scripture gives for the furtherance of the gospel to the glory of God.

Questions for discussion

1. Why is plural eldership (Acts 20:17; Titus 1:5) a blessing both for a local church and for the elders themselves.? Give some examples from your own church experience if you have them.

2. Discuss the responsibilities of elders in the life of the church (Acts 20:28; 1 Pet. 5:2). What benefit do they bring to the flock?

3. What kind of people should a church look for when they move to appoint an elder? (1 Tim. 3:1-7; Titus 1:6-9) How does that happen in your church?

4. How do godly deacons help gospel ministry flourish in the life of the church? (Acts 6:1-7; 1 Tim. 3:8-13)

5. Reflect on how the Lord has shepherded and cared for you through godly leaders in the past and thank God for them. Pray for your current elders and deacons, that they would continue to be godly in character and faithful as they teach and serve.

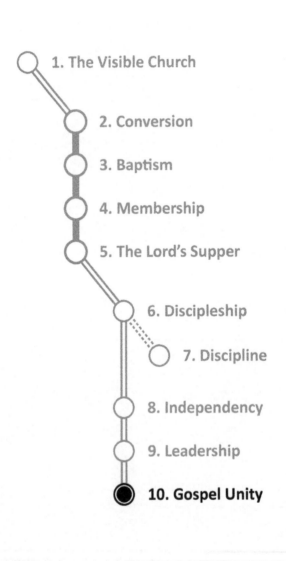

1. The Visible Church

2. Conversion

3. Baptism

4. Membership

5. The Lord's Supper

6. Discipleship

7. Discipline

8. Independency

9. Leadership

10. Gospel Unity

10. Gospel Unity

The blessings of inter-church fellowship
Paul Spear

10. *We believe that meaningful fellowship between local churches exists where there is evident faithfulness to the gospel, and that for the sake of displaying unity churches should look to foster good relationships with all other gospel-preaching churches within their locality.*

'Pastor, I love our church. From the moment I first came to Mums and Tots I have felt so welcome. I have learned so much and remembering the day of my baptism still makes me cry. I was wondering if we are getting involved in the bank holiday events with the other churches in the park. I hear that the Catholic tug of war team are favourites and that the Baptist church in town is looking for some reinforcements. It will be such good fun and such a good witness to all be working together.'

This was a real conversation. What would you have said? Your church may not participate in these sorts of events, but would this recently converted Christian understand why? In this example, the Baptist church in town would not claim to be evangelical. If it were evangelical, would that make a difference? Could your members explain to their friends why their church does not join in? After all, the pastor quotes all sorts of people in his sermons. He was trained at a mixed-denomination seminary and goes to conferences with people who are not Baptists! Our missionaries work with missionaries from other churches. Why don't we work with those churches here in the UK? Where is the consistency? When and where should we work with other churches?

This chapter starts with the independency of the local church, acknowledges the glory of the universal church and seeks to encourage fellowship, unity and co-operation between gospel churches.

The ecumenical tug of war is in fact slightly outside of my remit. The place I am operating in can be illustrated by the following diagram.

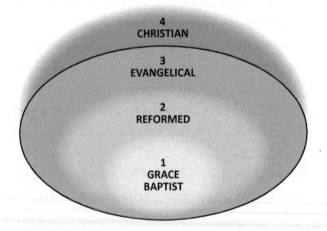

I want us to aim for some form of meaningful relationships with churches within groups 1, 2 and 3. Terms like evangelical and reformed will of course need to be defined. Biblical, gospel churches have lots of opportunities to fellowship with each other, first of all in their local[1] context and then with reference to wider connections.

The vital question of how to deal with those who are preaching error is not our subject. The question is instead how to work with those who are in Christ. We want to avoid the dangers of full-blooded ecumenism which compromises the gospel. We also want to avoid the dangers of hyper-critical isolationism. If our local church is like our immediate family, then other churches are like our extended family. Our aunties and uncles and cousins might do things a bit differently but we still love them and try to get along. I want to encourage fellowship and connectivity without compromising the integrity and independency of the local church.

This is both easy and difficult.

We have reasons for hope that pursuing fellowship with other churches might work. The Lord Jesus prayed for unity (John 17), so we can be confident that he is at work to bring it about. The Spirit dwells in all who are in Christ (1 Cor. 12:13; Rom. 8:9). We are already one in Christ (Rom. 6:1-5). This truth manifests itself in many ways. True gospel believers have a strong inclination to share fellowship together. Even the most

---

1 Local is a rather vague term and would change between city and rural contexts. I will leave it to your knowledge of your geography to decide what it means.

isolationist people I know have fellowship with someone. (Of course, they may be so isolationist as to be unknown to me or anyone else!)

Churches have sought to express unity together in history. This can be found in historic doctrinal standards:

- The First London Confession (1644) was explicit about the fellowship which should characterise churches: '...by all means convenient to have the counsel and help of another in all the needful affairs of the church...' (Article 47);

- The 1689 Baptist Confession exhorts churches '...to hold communion among themselves, for their peace, increase of love, and mutual edification.' In particular if a church or churches experience a time of difficulty, 'it is according to the mind of Christ, that many churches holding communion together, do, by their messengers, meet to consider, and give their advice in or about that matter in difference' (Article 26:14, 15);

- The 1966 Baptist Affirmation reminds likeminded churches that they 'have a responsibility to manifest their oneness in Christ in mutual fellowship and conference' (Article 7:7).

Principled positions on church unity are not just found in Baptist confessions:

- Chapters 26 and 31 of the Westminster Confession 'On the Communion of Saints' and 'Synods and Councils' outline a theological basis, a practical outworking and some limitations of church unity;

- Chapter 26 of The Savoy Declaration begins by identifying the universal church and chapter 27 'On the communion of the saints' is very similar to the statements in both the Westminster Confession and the 1689 Baptist Confession;

- The similarity in many core doctrines of the Westminster, Savoy and 1689 confessions is itself an encouragement to pursue co-operation and connection. They also help us to know where we must be honest and gracious about our differences.

Simple observation tells us that churches work together. This can operate at the institutional level, church to church, and often happens between church ministers. It also operates among individual members of different churches. When I began work as a teacher, one of my colleagues was a member of a similar church to my own. There was another evangelical from a different sort of church. Together we started a small Christian Union for the students. There were Baptists and Anglicans and Pentecostals (and even two slightly bemused girls from the Jehovah's Witnesses). We ate lunch, we read the Bible and we prayed, keeping the format very simple. It was not a church ministry as such but my church knew about it and prayed for me. The Lord was kind and good things resulted.

This type of fellowship happens at work or in neighbourhoods and all sorts of other places.

We can't stop ourselves from working together, and it is great!

However, difficulties can easily arise. The Christian world is full of divisions which we can't ignore. Within the evangelical or reformed spheres there are significant differences. Even Grace Baptist churches do not always get along. We have work to do. Some readers might consider that co-operation of any sort undermines the local church.

We need to be sure that what we are doing is based firmly in Scripture.

How New Testament churches were connected

The missionary church in Antioch (Acts 11:19-30; 15)

The church in Antioch was established by the missionary activities of the persecuted Christians from Jerusalem. The home church sent Barnabas to encourage the new church and to ensure that it was firmly founded in truth. He fetched Paul from Tarsus to help. The Antioch church then heard about the practical needs in Judea. Jerusalem shared their people, Antioch shared their cash![2] One of the key principles of independency is that the Lord provides for the needs of each church. One of the means he uses is other independent churches.

The relationship between the churches was not without

---

2   See 1 Corinthians 16:1-3; 2 Corinthians 8; 3 John 5-8; Romans 16:1.

difficulties. Acts 15 describes how one such difficulty was resolved. The controversy concerned the reception of the Gentiles into the churches. The chapter shows the issue and the solution. The relationship between the churches was preserved and nourished by the propositional truth of the gospel and by the outworking of gospel truth in a generous spirit. They were determined to treat people in a personal and gracious way even when dealing with foundational theological matters.

The connected churches in Galatia (Gal. 1:2, 22)

This group was comprised of local independent churches. They were accountable to the Lord Jesus through his word and would worship and be organised according to New Testament patterns. They were founded firmly in the doctrines of grace. They were linked to one another and not just by geography. Paul could send one letter to them all. A similar group existed in Judea (1:22).

They shared a common identity in Christ and were taught a true apostolic doctrinal standard. They understood that they were part of the universal church of which Christ is the head (3:26-29). They were called to love and serve those in the household of faith (6:10). They were to avoid those things which may cause harm and to seek to do one another good (5:13-15). The first application of this was within each church but there was surely an expectation that they would apply these principles between churches.

The Christ-centred churches of Revelation (Rev. 1–3)

John's vision in the early chapters of Revelation shows the presence of the Lord among his churches. Located in Asia Minor, the cities would have been linked by trade routes. Journeys between them would take a few days to a few weeks. Their spiritual experiences and condition are remarkably varied. Whatever their circumstances, they are connected in Christ. He was the Lord of each church and the link between them. He is the reason for our mutual care and concern. We are connected in Christ with the chapel up the road and to every fellowship across the world.

The multiple connections of the church in Rome (Rom. 16:1-16)

The church in Rome was greeted corporately by other churches and there were also close personal friendships. They were encouraged to welcome and help Phoebe who was from the church in Cenchrea. Priscilla and Aquila were commended for the help they gave to other churches. Paul had friends, fellow workers and family members in Rome. He had affection for the whole church and individuals within it.

The churches of 2000 years ago fostered good relationships with other gospel-preaching churches. They intentionally displayed gospel unity. We have ample reasons to imitate them.

Illustrating unity

I want to begin by thinking about how to do this through the use of some favourite illustrations of church unity.[3]

A garden enclosed

You will find walled gardens all over the UK, especially in parks and stately homes. If you want to look one up then the Alnwick Garden is one of the biggest and the best. In order to create a formal garden among surrounding woodland or parkland, a piece of ground, usually square, was enclosed by a wall. Shielded from the wind and intruders the garden would catch the rain and the warmth of the sun. This was the perfect environment for a flower garden or a kitchen garden to flourish. The church is a place of safety and beauty, tended by an expert gardener. There is only one way in and those inside are able to develop and grow. I want my garden to have safe and secure walls which are low enough so outsiders can see in. Several of my walls are actually party walls with other gardens/churches and there are plenty of places where we can chat across them or visit every so often. My main concern is to look after my own garden but I am always on the lookout for my neighbours and they are looking out for me.

If this is all a bit too Downton Abbey for your tastes then take the same idea to a suburban garden. The fence between you and your neighbouring church is low and you shake

---

3 I have known these images for a long time and I think they are widely known. I have no idea of the origin of any of them.

hands over it often. You even try to be kind to the slightly odd neighbour across the road.

The inkblots of fellowship

Each church is one drop of ink which spreads out from a dense and clear centre. The colours begin to separate, becoming more transparent as the ink spreads out. Other churches may be very close and have identically coloured theological ink and so our interactions are close. Other churches might be further away and colour things differently. The interactions will be weaker but may still be meaningful. As the ink spreads so the connections of the church with others become weaker and can even get a bit mixed with very different colours. There are some inkblots which are so far removed from us that we try to limit cross-contamination.

Ripples on a pond

Church interactions are like concentric ripples. They are larger nearer the centre and so our interactions will be stronger with those who are nearest to us. This nearness might be defined by geographical proximity, theological convictions, personal relationships or a combination of these and other factors. The imagery can be developed as each church has its own set of concentric circles which interact with other churches. There is interference when the circles cross. One church may have lots of different interactions at different distances from the centre. Churches may or may not have interactions in common. This can make principled inter-church fellowship look quite untidy at times but the complications are no reason not to keep rippling!

Ever decreasing circles

There is a cautionary alternative to the ripples. Churches face the hazard of a spiral of ever decreasing circles, a negative whirlpool of isolationism. This often begins with good intentions as we try to be wise in relationships and cautious about false teaching. The danger comes when being different becomes an end in itself. We find ourselves defending our theological identity and convictions through criticism and condemnation of others. We define ourselves by ever more specific theology and practice. As we pull up drawbridges and close doors we speak to a diminishing circle of people. They commend us for our faithfulness and congratulate us for being defenders of the truth. As the identity of the righteous is defined by being in my circle rather than by being in Christ, so a *de facto* heresy becomes true of the propositionally orthodox. We dream dreams of being Luther or Spurgeon, forgetting that they were often reluctant to pull away from other believers. When such churches become weak and isolated, the world, the devil or other Christians are to blame. Lack of fruitfulness becomes a sign that we must be truly of the elect – after all there are so few of us left! Anyone who challenges us is labelled as a heretic or a sell-out. Hypnotised by the downward spiral the church disappears into ineffectiveness and closure. This affliction is caused by a mixture of theological ineptitude, bad experiences and pride. This sort of isolationism should be identified and stopped at its early stages.

Ships in formation

Following that depressing interlude, allow me one final and favourite illustration. Each church is a ship on the wide ocean, heading for a promised destination. Each vessel is a battleship and a hospital ship rescuing those who are drowning after the shipwreck of their lives.[4] There is a command structure and every one of the ship's company plays their part. Those who are rescued are added to the crew. The ships are commanded by the First Lord of the Fleet who has given clear instructions about the nature of the mission and how each ship should be organised. They run free as the Spirit blows them forward but they also sail together in an enormous formation with common destiny and common purpose. They are aware that they are part of a giant task force but interact mostly with those who are close to them. They protect one another and share resources, even sending people to one another on occasions. They remind one another often of their joint mission and the orders coming from high command. Some ships lose their bearings and need help to get back on course. Some sadly turn aside completely or are sunk by heresy or sin. Some might have to be left behind as faithful ships must keep on course but only after every attempt at a rescue. The

4 Technically speaking they are already drowned as Adam Laughton's chapter reminds us, but this is just an illustration!

First Lord will lead each faithful ship home, some of them limping into port but often with flags waving and the sound of singing. What a day that will be!

Illustrations are fun, but for the more practically minded I would like to suggest a way to work out when and how we connect with other churches.

Practical unity

This proposal is built around two key virtues (love and truth), two key variables (purpose and boundaries) and two key practicalities (authority and accountability). These can help with all sorts of different scenarios.

Love and truth

In order for any meaningful expression of unity to happen we must love one another. Because God has a particular love for his children we have a particular love for them too. Because Christ has given his life for us we are willing to share generously. He has commanded that we love one another. The words of 1 Corinthians 13:4-7 are essential glue for any joint endeavour. We need patience and kindness as we get to know one another and learn about our differences and similarities. We exclude envy and arrogance as we seek to do the best for one another. We think well of one another and ensure that our actions and our words are constructive (Eph. 4:16). We don't get grumpy or upset too quickly as we remember we are all sinners saved by grace. We put the needs of others above our own, and while co-operation nearly always has mutual benefits, we are aiming to give more than we receive (Acts 20:35).

This love will grow as we get to know one another and work together. By meeting people personally we develop relationships. In the context of friendship we co-operate and build one another in faith. We might disagree on some things but we will refuse to fall out permanently. This has particular applications when facing a hostile world. We might have some disagreements but if we are attacked from the outside we link arms and stand together. We are family.

Church unity cannot be at the expense of the truth of the gospel. It must be an expression of the truth of the gospel. Catastrophic theological compromise is not the inevitable consequence of co-operation. It is worth reminding ourselves that we have an enemy who loves both error and disunity. We must be wise to his schemes and combat him on both fronts.

Some form of theological understanding and agreement is always necessary. This will help to identify our friends and fellow workers. It will show us the areas where we are of one accord and define a boundary beyond which we will try not to wander. Even this may not be straightforward. Because I believe in the doctrines of grace, I have a lot in common with people from other reformed churches even if they have a different view of baptism or church. Finding points of agreement is at least as important as understanding points of contention.

Purpose and boundaries

Each church should consider working through a decision-making process to determine the sort of relationships it will pursue as a body and how its members might interact with members of other churches.[5] We must consider principled boundaries built on truth. These will interact with the purpose of any expression of church unity.[6]

Referring back to the diagram earlier in this chapter, we might do different things with different groups. We might co-operate with quite a wide group if we agreed together on free speech or pro-life issues. My widest affiliation, for example, is with a group which meets to understand more about charity law and government legislation as it relates to churches. The theological basis of this is that the members self-identify as something resembling a Christian church or charity. The purpose is entirely practical and the theological boundary barely exists. This is not a gospel relationship!

We can often find gospel fellowship with other evangelicals in workplaces or student Christian Unions. The school CU mentioned above had a simple purpose: to teach the Bible to school students. We agreed on the authority of Scripture and the key truths of atonement and resurrection. Two of

5   Al Mohler outlined a system of theological triage which is a good place to begin thinking this through in more detail. See A.N. Mohler, 'A Call for Theological Triage in Christian Maturity', 20 May 2005, https://albertmohler.com [accessed 15/11/21]

6   Some of you may be aware of the illustration using bounded and centred sets. I chose not to use this as maths has the tendency to make people's eyes glaze over!

us involved in leading this would also have been reformed Baptists but the third was from a Pentecostal church. We could still work together.

The theological boundary changes again when considering a group such as Affinity.[7] Lots of different types of church are also affiliated to Affinity from across the whole of the UK. There is a theological statement we can agree on. We know what we do not agree on. We can still encourage and pray for one another and treat one another with gentleness and respect. Affinity works together on mission, social action and theological discussion. One of its key purposes is to express unity.

The boundary has to change again when working with the association to which my church belongs. Part of our aim is the promotion of a particular theological position. In this case the two variables are very closely linked.

Authority and accountability

Any co-operation might bump up against our convictions about the local church. Co-operating with another church inevitably means ceding a small amount of authority to one another. This leads to important questions. Can a church give up any of its authority? If it can, should it do so? Can any church act in a way which impacts the authority of another?

The answers to these questions are 'yes', 'yes' and 'yes', but only if each church understands how its own authority

---

7   See affinity.org.uk to find out more.

functions and has made a clear and principled decision about how accountability operates in any joint venture. Churches are independent under Christ. The Lord exercises his authority in the church through his word. The gathered church should base their decisions on what he has revealed and not simply on personal preferences and a majority vote. The authority of Christ also functions through the leaders of the church.[8] As they are identified and set aside for service they must lead by applying the Scriptures into specific circumstances. The gathered church has authority over its leaders even as it gives them authority in order for them to take decisions and lead. It is through these principled structures that the local church decides how it works with other churches.

Here we enter into questions about denominations, associations or partnerships. Concerns might rightly be expressed about the dangers of hierarchies, church politics and dominant personalities. Some are very cautious of formal associations which might try to influence or undermine the authority of the gathered local church. Others are very cautious of informal groupings dominated by a few men with little or no accountability. My proposed answer is threefold:

1. Identify what you are doing and why you are doing it;
2. Put in place clear pathways of authority and accountability for decision making so that something can actually get done;
3. Ensure that any project is clearly accountable to the

---

8 See chapter 8 on Independence and chapter 9 on Leadership.

churches involved so that they remain the primary point of human authority.

In order to get something done we sometimes have to let others take a lead. We may sacrifice our needs for the sake of others. We may, for example give resources for gospel work elsewhere, either near or far. Three churches may each have a plan and a proposal but resources may mean only two may progress. In a spirit of love and having identified common purpose and priorities one church may cancel or postpone its own project. Better to co-operate on two successful projects than to divide and accomplish nothing.

Some examples of meaningful fellowship, unity and co-operation

With these principles in place, we can serve together purposefully under Christ in all sorts of ways. This might include training, social action, evangelism, church planting or world mission.

I would like to illustrate how this can work using two scenarios from my own experience.

Working with teenagers

The youth work in my previous church experienced different phases. For several years we worked alongside another church which was reformed but not Baptist. The churches considered that a larger group where both teenagers and leaders were supported (purpose) was a good idea. There was a lot of gospel goodwill between the churches and lots of the adults and teenagers already knew each other (love). The content (boundaries of truth and practice) of the programme was agreed (authority). The youth leaders had freedom to run the programme under the oversight of elders from each church (accountability). This served a very useful purpose but ran its course as the dynamics of the two churches changed. It came to a natural end by mutual consent and these churches continue to express fellowship in other ways.

My church was also involved in a joint youth work with other Grace Baptist churches. This runs meetings six times each year plus a summer camp. Complementing the youth work of each church (purpose) this is particularly appreciated by churches with small groups. The churches share a common doctrinal foundation which defines the boundaries of the meetings (truth). A small committee is agreed by all of the churches in order to plan the meetings (authority and accountability). Other churches are invited to join in and gladly participate even though some of them are not Grace Baptists. This youth work continues to thrive and bear fruit.

Associating with other churches

Formal denominations which undermine the authority of the local church are not being proposed or supported here. I would distinguish these denominations from organisations like associations or gospel partnerships. By putting clear safeguards in place we can identify and avoid any potential pitfalls which undermine local church independence. Even though church co-operation will need some sort of organisation, the local church remains the core organisation for the gospel.

My former and current churches are members of an association. The aim of the churches is to affirm and uphold a doctrinal statement (truth); to mutually support one another through prayer and personal links (love); to help one another with practical ministries and to support one another in joint ventures in evangelism and church planting (purpose).

The theological DNA of the association includes clear convictions about the independence of the local church. There are structures in place to avoid undermining this (authority and accountability). Churches do not seek to impose their wills on one another and we are wary of an unhealthy dependence by any church on the central organisation (boundaries). While we do not encourage a revolving door approach to membership of the association, churches are free to leave at any time. If all the churches chose to stop associating in this way then the association would wind up its affairs and cease to exist. However, over time this association has increased in size as more likeminded churches choose to express gospel unity together. The organisational structure is based around the appointment of a committee by the churches. In order to avoid unhelpful centralisation the association churches organise themselves into smaller local districts.

Like any organisation it is far from perfect but the churches appreciate the mutual help which they can give and receive. Some of the shared expertise and resources which are administered through the association office are particularly appreciated. By associating together independent local churches have been saved from theological compromise, aided through times of turmoil, supported in pastoral appointments and training, advised on multiple practical matters and have worked together in church planting and revitalisation. Because the churches have strong principles guiding them they are able to maintain their independence while working with others in all sorts of contexts. All of these churches have other circles of fellowship as well. While there is a theological boundary there is also a lot of gospel goodwill and generosity to churches both inside and outside of the association.

Conclusion

I am aware that some readers might not be convinced by my examples. Some of you might be very cautious about formal associations. Others might have wanted me to push even stronger connections. I still want to be friends because we remain one in Christ. You can disagree with me about anything I have written in this chapter but I will try to treat you with gentleness and respect. To open God's word and discuss this robustly should not mean that we would fall out permanently even if I might find that hard. I cannot hope to promote unity, fellowship and co-operation while bearing grudges myself. Gospel generosity is required.

So what about the ecumenical tug of war competition in

the park? My church did not join in. The theological boundary was too wide and the purpose too vague. Some church members went along simply as individuals either out of curiosity or because of friendship with Christians who were joining in. Perfect consistency is always going to be tricky. On the other hand, some of the variables might change for another event. A genuine gospel opportunity might present itself within sensible boundaries. You all have opportunities for expressing unity with other churches. Take them whenever you can.

Questions for Discussion

1. How did independent churches express unity in the New Testament? Can you think of similar examples today? (Acts 11:19-30)
2. Which of the illustrations for church unity did you find most helpful? Why?
3. Which principles are most important to your church when you are deciding how much they to work with another church? (1 Cor. 15:1-11)
4. Pray for other churches in your area, for their faithfulness and fruitfulness in the gospel.

Conclusion

Andrew King

Throughout this book, we have written to try to persuade you that as our local churches more closely follow the Bible's order and structure they more clearly display the gospel and glorify God. Far more than mere Tourist Information Centres for the gospel, our churches are to be working communities where we live out all the glorious implications of the gospel. Pure churches of God.

Storied communities

Where is your neighbour likely to form her impressions about Christians and church? Probably from the common caricatures or stereotypes in the media. But how many positive portrayals of us will she find there? If our neighbour has been constantly fed a single negative story that shapes her understanding, we may understand why she is a little nervous about accepting our approaches.[1]

---

1 In another context, novelist Chimamanda Adichie warns that if we hear only a single story about another person or country, we risk a critical misunderstanding.

Yet here's the shocker: the Lord has entrusted *us* in our different churches to live out genuine displays of the gospel so that our neighbours can tangibly see the difference it makes to us! That is what we are taught by the apostle Peter:

> Once you were not a people, but now you are God's people; once you had not received mercy, but now you have received mercy. Beloved, I urge you as sojourners and exiles to abstain from the passions of the flesh, which wage war against your soul. Keep your conduct among the Gentiles honourable, so that when they speak against you as evildoers, they may see your good deeds and glorify God on the day of visitation. (1 Pet. 2:10-12)[2]

Bruce Riley Ashford writes, 'If we wish to make the gospel once again imaginable in our liberal society, we must offer a storied community which embodies its truth. And the church is this community, whose confession and members can make Christianity imaginable again.'[3]

We believe the joined-up practices argued for in this book provide the clearest biblical framework in which the gospel story can be embodied by each local church. It makes visible God's new community, providing the context in which believers can flourish and where love for God and neighbour can be cultivated.[4] No, we are not there yet, but surely the right structures and practices will help us all on our way towards being pure churches that display the gospel to our neighbours.

---

2 Scripture quotations in this chapter are ESV.

3 Collin Hansen (ed.), *Our Secular Age* (The Gospel Coalition, 2017).

4 I am thankful to Matt Benton for this observation.

Expat communities

An expatriate is a person temporarily or permanently living somewhere other than their native country. If you have ever lived in a different country you will know how important it is to gather with other expats to strengthen the common identity through shared stories and cultural activities.

We Christians are expats looking forward to the city that has foundations, whose designer and builder is God (Heb. 11:10). And so, another purpose of our local churches is to be our home from home. As we gather together and live out the biblical practices that define us and remind us who we are, so we are strengthened to remain faithful and increase in hope as we await the return of our Lord.

Unlike expat communities, losing our identity in Christ would be disastrous as we are not simply living within another friendly country but in real enemy territory. We are in exile and those around us demand that we conform to their beliefs and practices. Mike Cosper writes, 'when God's people are in exile we need to, among other things, rediscover and cultivate practices which reinforce who we are as the people of God'.[5] This is another reason why it is so important to be committed to the life of a local church. Gathering together is vital to our long-term spiritual wellbeing.

---

5   Mike Cosper, 'The Esther Option', 19 June 2018, https://www. thegospelcoalition.org/article/esther-option [accessed 15/11/21]

Show and tell

So, are our churches to be storied communities or expat communities? They are to be both. This is shown in Jesus' teaching in the Sermon on the Mount:

> You are the salt of the earth, but if salt has lost its taste, how shall its saltiness be restored? It is no longer good for anything except to be thrown out and trampled under people's feet. You are the light of the world. A city set on a hill cannot be hidden. Nor do people light a lamp and put it under a basket, but on a stand, and it gives light to all in the house. In the same way, let your light shine before others, so that they may see your good works and give glory to your Father who is in heaven. (Matt. 5:13-16)

Jesus was, first and foremost, teaching his disciples how they were now to live. They had entered the kingdom through repentance and faith and were called to live radically new lives. Of course, this manifesto statement would be more fully applied after Pentecost, but the call in the sermon was clear: you are now in the kingdom and that requires a radically new way of life.

The fact that the sermon 'you's are plural yet the definitions of salt and light are singular suggests a church application is intended. Of course, that includes each member, as the sum of the parts makes the whole.

You (plural) are the pure salt of the earth. You are now justified by faith in Christ Jesus and are set apart to be members of his kingdom, and you are to keep that purity. How then can a church include unbelievers as part of their number? Surely a logical application of this command to stay pure is to be careful who is brought in. And if someone openly sins and refuses to repent – how can they continue to have our backing without damaging the reputation of our King? This book has been making the case for membership of independent churches upon a clear profession of faith and obedience to the covenant sign of baptism.

You (plural) are the light of the world. Much of the rest of the Sermon on the Mount goes on to describe the character qualities and actions that show off the glorious holiness of God in his people: a community telling the story of humility, mourning over our sin yet hungering and thirsting to do and see righteousness; a people who, having received mercy and forgiveness, are becoming eager to pass this on to others and even to export it to those outside; people so convinced of the truth and majesty of their King that we become willing to suffer injustice and opposition for Christ in his name. Isn't that kind of community attractive to the outsiders looking for a better way to live?

Your local church is the light of your local world, a community desperate to treat each other with deep care; where lifelong marriage fidelity is prized; where truth has the highest stock value so that our words can be trusted; where we fight to put to death hypocrisy each day, and our giving and praying spring from honest hearts. Isn't that kind of community attractive? A community freed from the tyranny of chasing after money to buy fame and fortune. A people that can dare to rest because we know the future is safe in our Father's hands; where heart honesty leads to a careful hearing of each other and keeping our own house in order before challenging others. What an awesome vision for each of our local churches! Sure, we know painfully that we are still far from perfect, but isn't it our deepest desire to shine out this kind of life to those around us? As pure churches.

Of course, structure alone does not produce such a gloriously compelling community, but it does help. We believe that the ten chapters of this book work best when they are applied together.

In chapter 1, Jim reminded us that when a local church preaches the gospel it is the most eternity-shaping, heart-breaking, dead-raising, life-giving, heaven-empowered, grace-giving community there can ever be. And, as we let our church light shine out before others, they see our good works and are drawn by the preaching of the gospel to confess Christ themselves and give glory to our Father who is in heaven. This is the light we shine out.

In chapter 2, Adam showed that each true Christian has been converted. The Holy Spirit takes the gospel message and empowers it with life-giving power, to give us repentance towards God and faith in Jesus. We then became united to Christ by the Holy Spirit and this spiritual union forms the context for all our Christian life. If we belong to Jesus, then we belong to Christ's body, his church. Much of the light we are to shine out is the fruit of diverse gospel relationships in our local churches.

In chapter 3, David explained that while the act of baptising a Christian is not essential to their salvation, it is not unimportant. It is commanded by Christ and his command must be obeyed. Yet he also clarified that when a new disciple is baptised, *the church* affirms and accepts them on Christ's behalf. One way in which a local church keeps its saltiness is to collectively affirm only those who have been converted and are willing to publicly confess Christ in baptism.

In chapter 4, Jon showed that church membership draws the line between the church and the world. It identifies the Lord's people, saved by grace and bound together by their fellowship in the Lord Jesus Christ. This is deeply counter-cultural yet helps unite an outwardly diverse group to a deeply shared life. Without any clear way of knowing 'who is in', how will a local church be able to maintain its purity and thus keep shining brightly?

In chapter 5, Matt explained that the Lord's Supper is *more* than simply a meal for an individual Christian to take 'in communion' with the Lord. Rather, sharing the Supper together as a local church makes visible who God's people are in that time and place. Who are most fit to participate? Those who are clearly living together as God's people under his rule. This meal shows forth not only the gospel but its fruit: a united people living to display God's glory.

In chapter 6, I explained that a healthy church will have a culture of discipleship where all church members are disciples who are slowly and steadily built up by the other members. Yes, discipling includes teaching, but it also includes living everyday shared lives where various effects of the gospel are lived out and supported by the life of each local church.

Discipling brings glory to God and displays an increasingly Christ-like community to our friends and neighbours.

In chapter 7, Nigel showed that kind, loving, restorative, painful, healing, lifesaving, corrective, protective discipline is part of a healthy local church. It is sometimes necessary because our bridegroom's reputation is dirtied if his bride is unholy, and other members may also be tempted to follow suit. It is also a mark of love to the offender as it hopes for their repentance. Yet you cannot put someone out who has never been received in. We must guard our saltiness and stay pure.

In chapter 8, Mike explained that the New Testament gives clear commands and responsibilities to individual churches. If Christ expects such things of them, each church must have the *ability* to fulfil those *responsibilities*. Like cashiers in the bank who must recognise and reject the forged banknotes, by implication church members also have the responsibility of recognising and accepting the genuineness of new members, its teaching and its leaders. This helps maintain our saltiness.

In chapter 9, Brad argued that the local church should be led, taught and prayed for by a plurality of godly and gifted men serving as elders. Elders shepherd by teaching, praying, caring, serving and setting an example for the church, and they therefore need to know and be committed to a clearly identifiable flock. Local church membership clarifies who the elders lead, while local church independency enables each Spirit-filled member to hold their leaders biblically accountable.

In chapter 10, Paul suggested that if our local church is like our immediate family, then other churches are like our extended family. Our aunties, uncles and cousins might do things a bit differently, but we still love them and try to get along. With the accountability of independency, each of our churches can benefit from wider inter-church co-operation. In fact, independency needs this to avoid the danger of isolation. We shine out as networked lights across the world.

This collective 'box set' of ten interlocking aspects of church life are those practised by Grace Baptist churches (historically called 'Strict and Particular Baptist churches'). We commend them to you again, but not the historical name! Of course, *many* other churches hold to *much* of what this book has laid out. We hope what we have written has been generous and respectful yet has also helpfully explained our position. If your church already holds to all these things we hope you will be encouraged to press on with joy. Maybe you have now moved away from some of these aspects or have had different ways of doing things. We hope this book has made a clear and compelling case that will help you work towards making some structural and practical changes.

In his introduction, John Benton explained that when a church is doing what she is designed to do, something beautiful happens to which nothing on earth matches up: she becomes a united people living where the Lord himself delights to dwell. Isn't that what we long for? Not merely having our doctrines correctly lined up in a row, not simply being orthodox – but to be a people who know and enjoy the presence of the living God.

This fires us up to press on in our local churches. We are not merely building a house for the Lord, we are making a home where *he* dwells amongst us. Nothing on earth can beat knowing and enjoying life with God. And he makes his home amongst his people, in each of his precious churches. The structure and organisation of church life is how we make his home more as he wants it to be.

Press on, brothers and sisters: our labours are not in vain. We are building carefully because we are building for our Lord's pleasure. We are building joyfully because, as the Lord's redeemed people, we are guaranteed to enter into the joy of our Master.

> And I heard a loud voice from the throne saying, 'Behold, the dwelling place of God is with man. He will dwell with them, and they will be his people, and God himself will be with them as their God.' (Rev. 21:3)

Appendix

Covenant of Membership

Grace Baptist Church, Southport

The church is a fellowship of those who give themselves first to the Lord and then to one another. 2 Cor. 8:5.

The covenant of membership is an expression of acceptance of and commitment to the privileges and responsibilities that this entails. The covenant of membership is as follows:

We solemnly commit ourselves to the Lord and to one another in holy union and fellowship, promising humbly to submit ourselves to all duties required of us in Scripture.

We undertake, in the fear of the Lord, to observe the following things which we consider to be in accordance with the mind of Christ and necessary for the peace and well-being of the church.

i.   We will, with God's help and to the best of our ability, strive to live in holiness and brotherly love. John 15:17; Eph. 4:1-2; 1 Peter 1:14-16.

ii. We will, desiring each other's good, endeavour to stir up one another to love and good works, to assist one another in all our varied circumstances and spiritual states;

bearing one another's weaknesses and failings with tenderness and compassion; and to warn and rebuke one another with all humility and affection. Rom. 12:10, 15:1-2; Gal. 6:2; Eph. 4:2; 1 Thess. 5:14; Heb. 10:24-25.

iii. We will, in a special manner, be concerned to pray for one another, for the increase and spiritual prosperity of the church, for the presence of Christ to be manifest in it and for the pouring of God's Spirit upon it, and his protection over it to his glory. Luke 11:13; Acts 12:5; 2 Thess. 3:1; James 5:16.

iv. We will strive together for the truth of the gospel and purity of God's ways and ordinances, to avoid causes, and deal appropriately with causers, of division, endeavouring to keep the unity of the Spirit in the bond of peace. Rom. 16:17; Eph. 4:3; 2 Tim. 2:23; Titus 3:9-11; 2 John 7-11.

v. We will meet together on Lord's Days for worship and at other times as we have opportunity to encourage one another by our own attendance at the meetings of the church, to serve and glorify God in his worship, to observe the ordinance of the Lord's Supper, to edify one another and to gather to pray for the spiritual prosperity of the church. Rom. 1:11-12, 15:2; 1 Cor. 11:24-26; Heb. 10:25, 13:15.

vi. We will pray for and encourage the pastors and officers of the church in the discharge of their duty and be loyal to them as long as they shall follow the gospel of grace, uphold the doctrines contained in the articles of faith and maintain a godly example in their personal life. 1 Thess. 5:12-13; Heb. 13:7, 17-19.

vii. We will endeavour to be faithful stewards of all God's gifts to us and in a responsible manner to provide financially for the work of the church, the support of the ministers of the word, the upkeep of the place of worship, the relief of the needy, especially those within the church, and the maintenance of missionary work. Prov. 3:9; Mal. 3:10; 1 Cor. 16:2; 2 Cor. 8:1-4, 9:7; Gal. 6:6; Phil. 4:15-17.

These and all other duties to be found in the word of God we desire to submit to humbly and to practise through the gracious help of the Holy Spirit, being conscious of our weakness, whilst we give ourselves in love to God who has called us into his grace and made us his children.

Further Resources

Chapter 6: Discipleship

- Barry Cooper, *Discipleship Explored* (Good Book Company, 2018).
- Bobby Jamieson, *Growing One Another: Discipleship in the Church* (Crossway/9Marks, 2012).
- Ken Smith, *With Him* (10Publishing, 2017).
- Graham Beynon, *God's New Community* (IVP, 2005).
- Bruce Milne, *Know the Truth* (IVP, 2014).
- Eric Wright, *Church – No Spectator Sport* (Evangelical Press, 1994).
- J. I. Packer and G. A. Parrett, *Grounded in the Gospel* (Baker Books, 2010).

Chapter 7: Discipline

- Wayne Grudem, *Systematic Theology* (IVP, 1994) 894-900.
- Jeremy Kimble, *40 Questions about Church Membership and Discipline* (Kregel, 2017).

Chapter 9: Leadership

- Mark Dever and Paul Alexander, *The Deliberate Church* (Crossway, 2005).
- D. A. Carson, *Memoirs of an Ordinary Pastor: The life and reflections of Tom Carson* (Crossway, 2008).
- Charles Bridges, *The Christian Ministry* (first published 1830) (reprinted Banner of Truth, 1959).
- Jeramie Rinne, *Church Elders: How to Shepherd God's People like Jesus* (Crossway, 2014).
- Mike McKinley, *Church Planting is for Wimps* (Crossway/9Marks, 2016).
- Richard Baxter, *The Reformed Pastor* (first published 1656) (reprinted Banner of Truth, 2007).

Works Cited

Adiche, Chimamanda, 'The Danger of a Single Story', TED*Global* 2009, July 2009, <www.ted.com/talks/chimamanda_adichie_the_danger_of_a_single_story?> (last accessed 15 November 2021).

Allison, Gregg R., *Sojourners and Strangers: The Doctrine of the Church* (Wheaton: Crossway, 2012).

Bargerhuff, Eric, *The Love that Rescues: God's Fatherly Love in the Practice of Church Discipline* (Eugene: Wipf & Stock, 2010).

Baxter, Richard, *The Reformed Pastor* (Edinburgh: The Banner of Truth Trust, 1656, reprt. 2007).

Beale, Greg, *1-2 Thessalonians* (Leicester: IVP, 2003).

Bellah, Robert, Richard Madsen, William Sullivan, Ann Swidler and Steven Tipton, *Habits of the Heart: Individualism and Commitment in American Life* (Berkeley: University of California Press, 1985).

Calvin, John, *Institutes of the Christian Religion*, 4.17.10.

Carter, Tom (ed.), *Spurgeon at His Best* (Grand Rapids: Baker, 1988).

Chambers, Ralph, *The Strict Baptist Chapels of England*, Vol 1 (Rushden, 1952).

Cosper, Mike, 'The Esther Option', 19 June 2018, <www.thegospelcoalition.org/article/esther-option> (last accessed 15 November 2021).

Garland, David E., *New American Commentary on 2 Corinthians* (Nashville: B&H Publishers, 1999).

Grudem, Wayne, *Systematic* Theology (Leicester: IVP, 1994).

Hansen, Collin (ed.), *Our Secular Age: Ten Years of Reading and Applying Charles Taylor* (Deerfield: The Gospel Coalition, 2017).

Hooker, Richard, *Laws of Ecclesiastical Polity*, Book 3.

Hoole, Charles H., trans. Didache 9:5 <https://www.earlychristianwritings.com/text/didache-hoole.html> (accessed 12/06/18).

Hull, Bill, *The Complete Book of Discipleship: On Being and Making Followers of Christ* (Carol Stream: Navpress, 2006).

Hulse, Erroll, 'The Implications of Baptism', in *Local Church Practice* (Carey Publications, 1978).

Jamieson, Bobby, *Going Public* (Nashville: B&H Academic, 2015).

Jamieson, Bobby, *Understanding Baptism* (Nashville: B&H Academic, 2016).

Jamieson, Bobby, *Understanding the Lord's Supper* (Nashville: B&H Academic, 2018).

Kimble, Jeremy M., *40 Questions about Church Membership and Discipline* (Grand Rapids: Kregel, 2017).

Kingdon, David, *Children of Abraham* (London: Grace Publications, 2021).

Klappert, Bertold, 'Lord's Supper', in C Brown (ed.), *New International Dictionary of New Testament Theology*, Vol 2, (Grand Rapids: Zondervan, 2008).

Leeman, Jonathan, *Church Discipline* (Wheaton: Crossway, 2012).

Leeman, Jonathan, *Church Membership* (Wheaton: Crossway/9Marks, 2012).

Leeman, Jonathan, *Political Church* (Downers Grove: IVP Academic, 2016).

Leeman, Jonathan, *The Church and the Surprising Offence of God's Love* (Wheaton: Crossway/9Marks, 2010).

Leeman, Jonathan, 'The Preemptive Resignation—A Get Out of Jail Free Card?', 25 February 2010, <www.9marks.org/article/preemptive-resignation-get-out-jail-free-card> (last accessed 15 November 2021).

Leithart, Peter, *Blessed are the Hungry: Meditations on the Lord's Supper* (Moscow: Canon Press, 2000).

Leithart, Peter, *The Kingdom and the Power, Rediscovering the Centrality of the Church* (Phillipsburg: P&R Publishing, 2012).

Lloyd Jones, D. Martyn, *Knowing the Times* (Edinburgh: The Banner of Truth Trust, 1989).

Masters, Peter, *Church Membership in the Bible* (London: The Wakeman Trust, 2008).

McCracken, Brett, 'Church Shopping with Charles Taylor', in Collin Hansen (ed.), *Our Secular Age: Ten Years of Reading and Applying Charles Taylor* (Deerfield: The Gospel Coalition, 2017).

McCracken, Brett, *Uncomfortable: The Awkward and Essential Challenge of Christian Community* (Wheaton: Crossway, 2017).

McLuhan, Marshall and Quentin Fior, *The Medium is the Message* (London: Penguin, 1967).

Mohler, A. N., 'A Call for Theological Triage and Christian Maturity', 20 May 2004, <https://albertmohler.com/2004/05/20/a-call-for-theological-triage-and-christian-maturity-2> (last accessed 15 November 2021).

Morris, Leon, *The Gospel According to John* (Grand Rapids: Eerdmans, 1971).

Murray, Iain H., *The Reformation of the Church: A Collection of Reformed and Puritan Documents on Church Issues* (Edinburgh: The Banner of Truth Trust, 1965).

Murray, John, *Redemption* (Grand Rapids: Eerdmans, 1955).

Needham, Nick, 2000 Years of Christ's Power: The age of the early church fathers, Vol 1 (Christian Focus/Grace Publications, 2016).

Newton, Phil A., Elders in Congregational Life: Rediscovering the Biblical Model for Church Leadership (Grand Rapids: Kregel Publications, 2005).

O'Donovan, Oliver, Desire of the Nations: Rediscovering the Roots of Political Theology (Cambridge: Cambridge University Press, 1996).

Packer, J. I. and G. A. Parrett, Grounded in the Gospel: Building Believers the Old-Fashioned Way (Grand Rapids: Baker Books, 2010).

Rinne, Jeramie, Church Elders: How to Shepherd God's People like Jesus (Wheaton: Crossway, 2014).

Rutledge, Arthur B., 'Evangelistict Methods in Acts', Southwestern Journal of Theology, Vol 17 (Fall 1974).

Schreiner, Patrick, The Kingdom of God and the Glory of the Cross (Wheaton: Crossway, 2018).

Schreiner, Thomas D. and Shawn D. Wright, (eds.), Believer's Baptism: Sign of the New Covenant in Christ (Nashville: B&H Academic, 2006).

Stein, Robert H., 'Baptism and becoming a Christian in the New Testament', SBJT 2 (1998), 6-17.

Stott, John, The Letters of John (Leicester: IVP, 2003).

Trueman, Carl, Grace Alone: Salvation as a Gift of God (Grand Rapids: Zondervan, 2017).

Verbrugge, Verlyn D., New International Dictionary of New Testament Theology (Grand Rapids: Zondervan, 2003).

Ware, Bruce, 'Believer's Baptism View' in David F. Wright (ed.), Baptism: Three Views (Carol Stream: IVP, 2009).

White, John, and Ken Blue, Church Discipline That Heals: Putting Costly Love into Action (Carol Stream: IVP, 1992).

Contributors

John Benton was trained in science, gaining a D.Phil. He was a pastor in Guildford for over thirty-five years in which, despite his enormous failings, the Lord blessed the church. John was for many years managing editor of *Evangelicals Now* and is the author of many books, including his recent title, *Resilient*, which is about perseverance in Christian leadership. He is currently Director for Pastoral Support at the Pastors' Academy based at London Seminary. He is happily married to Ann, the love of his life, and together they have four children, all Christians and married to Christians – a source of enormous joy.

Matthew Benton taught Economics and Politics for ten years before studying for a M.Div. at Trinity Evangelical Divinity School in the US. Returning to the UK, he served as a pastor in training at Emmanuel Church, Leamington Spa, for two years. Since 2015 he has been part of the ministry team at Limes Avenue Baptist Church in Aylesbury, first as the assistant pastor and now as the pastor. Matt is married to Chrisi and they have three children. He would argue that life is better for good coffee, good books and sport.

Brad Franklin serves as the pastor of St Giles Christian Mission in Islington. As Brad is the father of six boys and a girl, he has very little spare time. In the bit he does have, you may find him eating Greek food, reading old theology books, supporting Tottenham Hotspur, or running a lot slower than he used to. Brad is married to Naomi.

After a law degree and fifteen years in primary school teaching, **Nigel Graham** studied at London Seminary for two years. In 2007 he became the pastor of Warboys Baptist Church, near Huntingdon. He is married to Rebecca and they have three grown up children and a Maine Coon cat. Nigel enjoys history (particularly American history), politics and an occasional (and often frustrating) round of golf.

Mike Gilbart-Smith is married to Hannah and they have six children. He is the pastor of Twynholm Baptist Church in Fulham, London. Previously he was assistant pastor at Capitol Hill Baptist Church, Washington DC, and at Farnham Baptist Church, Surrey. He teaches as a visiting lecturer in New Testament at London Seminary, and writes occasionally for 9marks.org.

Andrew King is married to Lena and they have two daughters. He is co-pastor at Highbury Baptist Church in central north London and also serves as Association Secretary for AGBC(SE). Before that he was a senior lecturer in engineering design at the University of Bristol. He is the author of *Be Bright – living for Christ at University*.

Adam Laughton taught as a maths teacher for five years, before serving for eleven years as co-pastor of Grace Baptist Church, Southport. He is now the pastor of Grace Church Ebbsfleet. He is married to Julia and together they have four children. He enjoys modern board games (which he sometimes inflicts on his family) and, when possible, walking in places like the Lake District.

Jim Sayers comes from Surrey. After studying law in Aberystwyth, he trained for ministry in Edinburgh, and served as assistant pastor at Hook Evangelical Church. He was pastor of Kesgrave Baptist Church in Suffolk for fourteen years, and for eleven years he served as Communications Director of Grace Baptist Mission. He now leads a church plant, Grace Church Didcot in South Oxfordshire. He is married to Helen and they have three adult children. He is also chairman of Praise Trust.

David Skull studied civil engineering at university and worked in the water industry. He served as a UCCF Staff Worker before training for ministry at Oak Hill College. At the time of writing he was Pastor of Grace Church Guildford but is now helping to lead Grace Church Brighton - a new city plant. He is married to Naomi and they have four children.

Born and bred in Bristol, **Paul Spear** was converted at Warwick University. He taught maths in Southwark before being sent to Bible College in Bridgend with overseas mission in mind. However, he ended up serving in the UK, first in Tooting and then for fifteen years in Hemel Hempstead. He is now the Pastoral Dean at Union School of Theology. He is happily married to Fiona and they have three grown-up children. They now live in Bridgend.

Jonathan Stobbs is pastor of Penzance Baptist Church where he has served since 2008. Prior to that, he was a secondary school history teacher, after completing a history degree at Royal Holloway, University of London. He is married to Jenna and they have three children. Jonathan enjoys any type of sport, particularly football, and in the past has represented Great Britain in fencing.

Also by Grace Publications

Association

Edited by Ryan King & Andrew King

The New Testament is filled with imagery illustrating co-operative efforts of Christian individuals within their local church. But what about relationships between churches?

Association makes the case that more can be done together, as local churches associate for fellowship and mission.

With contributions by James M. Renihan, Robert Strivens, Greg Tarr, Paul Smith, Nigel Hoad, Barry King, Leonardo De Chirico, Jaime D. Caballero, and John Benton.

Available to buy from gracepublications.co.uk

Also by Grace Publications

Children of Abraham
David Kingdon

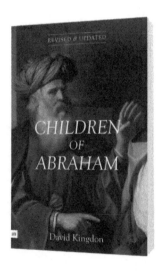

First published during a resurgence of interest in Reformed theology, David Kingdon's classic defence of believer's baptism made a major contribution to the re-thinking of the doctrine of the church and baptism around the world. Now revised and updated, this new edition features two previously unpublished chapters.

'The best brief treatment of the topic.'
D.A. Carson

'The definitive study of a Reformed defence of believer's baptism.'
Michael Haykin

Available to buy from gracepublications.co.uk